THE MEDIEVAL LIBRARY UNDER
THE GENERAL EDITORSHIP OF
SIR ISRAEL GOLLANCZ, Litt.D., F.B.A.

The works consulted include the following :

Hrotsvithæ Opera : Edited by PAUL WINTERFELD.

Hrotsvithæ Opera : Edited by H. L. SCHURZFLEISCH.

Hrotsvithæ Opera : Edited by CONRAD CELTES (Nürnberg, 1501).

Patrologiæ Cursus Completus : J. P. MIGNE (vol. 137).

Abraham : Translated into French by C. CUZIN, with critical preface.

Thêâtre de Roswitha : CHARLES MAGNIN.

Origines du thêâtre Moderne : CHARLES MAGNIN.

Antiquitates Gandersheimensis : LEUCKFELD.

Six Medieval Women : ALICE KEMP WELCH.

———

I am much indebted to Dame Laurentia McLachlan, O.S.B., Superioress of Stanbrook Abbey, and to the Reverend Paul Bonnet of Lyons University, for assistance in the work of translation.—CHRISTOPHER ST. JOHN.

THE PLAYS OF ROSWITHA

ROSWITHA PRESENTING HER PANEGYRIC OF OTHO THE GREAT TO OTHO II IN
THE PRESENCE OF THE ABBESS GERBERG.

From the woodcut by DÜRER.

THE PLAYS OF
ROSWITHA TRANSLATED
BY CHRISTOPHER ST. JOHN
WITH AN INTRODUCTION BY CARDINAL
GASQUET AND A CRITICAL PREFACE BY
THE TRANSLATOR

Hrotsvit, of Gandersheim
...

Benjamin Blom
New York

INTRODUCTION

By HIS EMINENCE CARDINAL GASQUET

WHATEVER may be thought of the precise merits of these six short dramas, now translated into English for the first time,* it will be conceded that a collection of plays bearing the date of the 10th century, authenticated as the work of a woman, and a nun, is a remarkable phenomenon, interesting to students of monasticism and of the drama alike.

At one time, it is interesting to note, it was suggested that the author of these dramas was an Englishwoman. In fact, the English scholar, Laurence Humfrey, who first introduced them to notice in this country, endeavoured to prove that Roswitha was no other than St. Hilda of Northumbria. His theory cannot, of course, be maintained; but the very anxiety shown to identify this talented poetess and dramatist as a native of this country is evidence of the high estimation in which her compositions were held in the 16th century,

* Since this was written, an English translation of one of the plays, *Abraham*, has been issued by a private press.

72000

the time when Laurence Humfrey, an exile from England for his religion, learnt to know them in Germany. It is now an established fact that the plays are the work of a Benedictine nun of Gandersheim, in Saxony, and their merits certainly justify her biographer's exclamation : " Rara avis in Saxonia visa est."

It used to be assumed that between the 6th and the 12th century all dramatic representations ceased, but each of these centuries when patiently searched has yielded some dramatic texts. The feudal period, reckoned the most barbarous, and Germania, set down then, as later in history, as the least civilized of countries, have produced the most considerable and least imperfect of these texts in the plays of Hrotsuitha, or Roswitha, a nun of the Order of St. Benedict, who spent her religious life in the Convent of Gandersheim.

There is a marked difference between her plays and such dramas as *The Mystery of the Wise and Foolish Virgins*, which is little more than an amplification of the sequence of the liturgy. We find here an author familiar not only with the Scriptures, the works of the Fathers of the Church, of the agiographers, and of the Christian philosophers, but with Plautus, Terence, Horace, Virgil, and Ovid—an author who, on her own confession, took the theatre of Terence as her model.

The Abbey of Gandersheim, where these plays were written, was founded about the year 850 by Ludolph, Duke of Saxony, at the request of his wife Oda, a

Frankish princess. Although these were what men call "the dark ages," the darkness was comparative. The Saxon court at this time was enlightened, and the Abbeys of Saxony, notably that of Corbei, were centres of learning and civilization. Gandersheim was one of the "free abbeys," that is to say its Abbess held it direct from the King. Her rights of overlordship extended for many miles ; she had her own law courts, and sent her men-at-arms into the field. In fact, she enjoyed the usual privileges and undertook the usual responsibilities of a feudal baron, and as such had the right to a seat in the Imperial Diet. Coins are extant, struck by the Abbesses of Gandersheim, whose portraits they bear.

During the 10th and 11th centuries these Abbesses were drawn chiefly from the royal house of Saxony, which had been raised to the dignity of the Imperial throne of Germania. Leuckfeld, in his voluminous history of Gandersheim, quotes a contemporary chronicler who praises the royal nuns for keeping all luxury and state out of the life of the community, and for observing the Rule of St. Benedict strictly. " They were forbidden," says the chronicler, " to eat away from the common table at the appointed times, except in case of sickness. They slept together, and came together to celebrate the canonical hours. And they set to work together whenever work had to be done." The Abbess who ruled the community in Roswitha's time was Gerberg, or Gerberga, a niece of the Emperor Otho I.

Gerberg was a good classical scholar, and Roswitha tells us, in one of the introductory prefaces with which, fortunately for posterity, her works are freely sprinkled, how much she owed to the tuition of this Abbess, " younger in years than I, but far older in learning."

It is from such sentences as this that we are able to gain a little information about Roswitha's life. Her mention of certain historical events and personages proves that she was born after the year 912 and before the year 940 (the known date of Gerberg's birth). She seems to have entered the religious life at Gandersheim when she was about twenty-three years old. She tells us nothing about her antecedents, but as Gandersheim was an exclusive house we may assume that she was of gentle birth. What education or experience of the world she had had before she became a nun is a matter of guesswork.

Roswitha wrote in Latin, the only language used in the 10th century in the West for literary composition. Conrad Celtes, the well-known humanist, discovered the manuscript, the writing of which cannot be earlier than the 9th, or later than the 10th century, in the library of the Benedictine monastery of St. Emmeran, Ratisbon, in the last days of the 15th century. In the year 1501 it was printed. This first edition has an interesting frontispiece representing the nun poet and dramatist presenting her works to the Emperor Otho II, in the presence of her Abbess Gerberg, who wears the crown

of a " Fürstäbtin." This and the other plates illustrat-
ing incidents in the plays have been attributed to both
Dürer and Cranach, but they are not signed. Another
edition, that of Schurzfleisch, in nearly all respects a
reprint of the first, was issued in 1707, augmented with
biographical and philological notes. The text given in
the Latin Patrology (Migne, Tomus 137) is taken
from the Schurzfleisch edition. More valuable to the
student is Magnin's edition. The French commentator
collated the Celtes and Schurzfleisch texts with the
original manuscript, which in 1803 had been moved
from St. Emmeran to the Munich library, and found
one or two readings preferable to those of Celtes.
Magnin also restored some stage directions omitted by
Celtes, one of which, in the eighth scene of *Callimachus*,
affords, as the English translator notes, valuable evidence that the play was acted, or at least intended for
representation.

The original manuscript is divided into three parts.
The first contains eight poems or metrical legends of
the Saints in which reliable authorities are carefully
followed, much skill being shown, however, in the
arrangement of the material and in the handling of
the " leonine hexameter." The second part consists of
the six plays here given in English; the third, of a long
unfinished poem called " Panegyric of the Othos." Celtes
changed the order, which is to be regretted, as it is
obviously chronological. Roswitha's preface to Part III

shows more confidence than the preface to the plays, and
very much more than the diffident preface to the poems.
One of these poems, " Passio Sancti Pelagii," once enjoyed
a very high reputation, and is often quoted by Spanish
and Portuguese agiographers. The Bollandists print it
entire in the *Acta Sanctorum*. It has another interest in
that Roswitha tells us that she obtained her facts from a
witness of the saint's martyrdom.

Although Roswitha claims Terence as her master in the
art of play-writing, it cannot be said that she imitates him
closely. When *Paphnutius* was acted in London in 1914
the dramatic critic of *The Times* was justified from one
point of view in asserting that Roswitha's style is " not in
the least Terentian." For one thing she is quite indifferent to the " unities," and transports us from place
to place with bewildering abruptness. Her relation to
Terence, as she herself insists, is one of moral contrasts
rather than of literary parallels. The " situation " in
Terence's comedies almost invariably turns on the frailty
of women ; in Roswitha's plays as invariably on their
heroic adherence to chastity. Although considerable
variety is shown in the treatment of each story, the motive
is always the same—to glorify uncompromising fidelity to
the vow of virginity. This nun dramatist deals coura-
geously, but, it must be added, delicately, when it is
remembered that she lived in an age when even the best
educated were neither fastidious nor restrained in manners
or conversation, with the temptations which her characters

overcome. The preface to her plays shows that it was not without some qualms of conscience that she wrote of things " which should not even be named among us." But the purity of her intentions, which was obviously recognized by her religious superiors, should induce the most prudish reader to refrain from charges of impropriety. With all their shortcomings, Roswitha's works have a claim to an eminent place in medieval literature, and do honour to her sex, to the age in which she lived, and to the vocation which she followed.

THE PLAYS OF ROSWITHA*

By CHRISTOPHER ST. JOHN

THIS translation of the six plays of Roswitha (there are
really seven, for the two parts of *Gallicanus* practically
constitute two separate dramas) was begun in the year
1912 and completed in 1914. The lively interest provoked by the stage performance of one of the translations
(that of the play *Paphnutius*) by the Pioneer Players in
January 1914 led me to think that the publication of the
whole theatre of Roswitha in English would be welcomed
by all students of the drama. Unfortunately, the war
delayed publication, and the manuscript was entirely
destroyed by a fire at the publisher's premises in Dublin
during the Irish insurrection of Easter 1916.

The work of collating the various Latin texts of
Roswitha's plays and producing a translation which should
preserve some of the naive simplicity of the original had
been a difficult one, and to begin it all over again was a
heart-breaking task. The consciousness that the interest
in Roswitha provoked by the performance of *Paphnutius*

---

* I have adopted this form of the name in preference
to "Hrotsuitha," "Hrotswitha," or "Hrosvitha," as
being more easily pronounced and more pleasant to the
eye. The name is said to be derived from the old Saxon
word "Hrodsuind" (strong voice), a derivation accepted
by Roswitha herself in her preface to her plays, when
she writes "ego, clamor validus Gandeishermensis,"
and approved by Grimm.

had waned did not alleviate the heaviness of spirit in which the work of replacing the burned manuscript was undertaken.

Those readers who are unable or unwilling to compare the translations with the original should be warned that Roswitha's dialogue is characterized by a simplicity and conciseness hardly attainable in any tongue but Latin. The difficulty of finding equivalents for the terse phrases employed tempts the translator to " write them up." Although I have aimed at producing a readable translation for lovers of the drama in all its forms rather than an exact paraphrase for scholars, I have tried to resist this temptation at the risk of making the dialogue seem at times almost ludicrously bald. Except in a few cases where the use of " thou " seemed dramatically fit, " tu " has been rendered by " you." Roswitha's style is colloquial, and the constant employment of the singular pronoun would misrepresent its character. The Latin is not obsolete, and it would surely be a mistake to translate it into an obsolete vernacular. Although the author's syntax is decadent, and there is a tendency to make every sentence analytical, her use of words is classical, and her Latin in this respect superior to the scholastic Latin of the Middle Ages. The only principle observed in my translation has been the general one laid down by Edward Fitzgerald : " The live dog is to be preferred to the dead lion—in translation at any rate," and if this has involved a loss of dignity, I hope there may be some compensating

gain in ease and force.*   In regard to the names of
the characters in the plays, when there were well-
known English equivalents such as "Hadrian" and
"Constantine" I have not hesitated to use them, but
when there were none I have given the Latin names.
There is a good precedent for this inconsistency.   We
speak of "Rome" and "Venice," but we do not try to
Anglicize Perugia or Assisi.

The plays are all founded on well-known legends,
which Roswitha follows very closely as regards the facts.
But she shows great originality in her use of the facts
and in her development of characters often merely
indicated in the legends.   Three of the plays, *Gallicanus*,
Dulcitius, and *Sapientia*, deal with the conflict between
infant Christianity and Paganism, martyrdoms under the
Emperors Hadrian, Diocletian, and Julian the Apostate
being the chief incidents.   *Gallicanus*, which comes first
in the manuscript, shows considerable skill in dramatic
construction.   Incident follows rapidly on incident.   The
scene lies alternately in Rome and on the battlefield, yet
the action is kept quite clear.   The story is easily followed,
although Roswitha, like all good dramatists, eschews
narrative.   Gallicanus, one of the Emperor Constantine's
generals, claims the hand of the Emperor's daughter as a
reward for undertaking a dangerous campaign against the

* Believing that the representation of the plays is
possible, even desirable, I have also aimed at making the
dialogue *speakable*.

Scythians. The Emperor knows that Constance has taken a solemn vow of chastity, but he dares not offend Gallicanus by a refusal, on account of the value of his military services. So he temporizes, and consults Constance, who shows great shrewdness in dealing with the situation. She sends her almoners, John and Paul, to accompany Gallicanus on the Scythian expedition, in the hope that they will convert him to Christianity before he returns to marry her. The stratagem succeeds. Gallicanus, saved from defeat at a critical moment in the battle by the intervention of a heavenly host, becomes a Christian, and on his return to Rome shows respect for Constance's resolution to remain in the virgin state, and renounces her. But he admits that the renunciation is bitter—Roswitha often shows such touches of sympathy with natural human desires—and we are made to feel that, although the dramatist was in no doubt that the life of chastity, poverty, and obedience is the highest life, she understood how hard it is for those who embrace it to believe that the yoke will be easy and the burden light.

The second play, *Dulcitius*, is poorly constructed and, as a whole, less interesting than any of the plays. Yet it has some features which repay close study. It is the only play of Roswitha's obviously designed to provoke laughter, and if the level of the opening scenes had been maintained would be a very droll religious farce. Here we have the usual tale of martyrdom interspersed with incidents of buffoonery. The conventional cruel and bloody executioners are replaced by comic soldiers and a comic governor. Unfortunately, the farcical vein is suddenly abandoned, perhaps because Roswitha's Abbess thought such fooling undignified in a nun ! There must be some explanation of the sudden disappearance of the comic character of Dulcitius from the play. However, even as it stands *Dulcitius* is worth a great deal, since it affords the best proof we have that Roswitha's plays were written for representation. There is indirect proof in the fact that we know that plays were acted at Gandersheim, as at other monasteries, on great occasions, but here is direct evidence. All the fun of *Dulcitius* lies in the action. No dramatist who had not in mind the effect on *spectators* could have conceived the scene in which the foolish governor, black as a sweep from his amorous encounter with the kitchen pots and pans which he mistakes for young women, is chased away from the palace gates, asking the while if there is anything amiss with his fine and handsome appearance. Stage directions, or *didascalia*, are very rarely found in old dramatic texts, but when Magnin compared Roswitha's original text * with the first printed edition he found several which had been omitted by Celtes.

Callimachus, *Abraham*, and *Paphnutius* precede

* The manuscript is now in the Munich City Library. Recently another manuscript, containing four of the six dramas, is reported to have been discovered among the state archives of Cologne. (*Times* Berlin Correspondent, May 9, 1922.)

Sapientia in the manuscript, but as the last belongs by reason of its subject to the same group as *Gallicanus* and *Dulcitius*, it is more convenient to discuss it next. It is the best constructed of the " martyrdom " plays, and is singled out for special praise by most of the Roswitha commentators. The final scene in which Sapientia, having buried the bodies of her martyred children outside Rome, lifts up her soul in an ecstatic prayer for death is described by Magnin as " a ray of Sophocles shining through a Christian mind." Many, however, may find the repetition in the long-drawn-out " torture " scenes monotonous, and the impertinence of Sapientia's daughters to their imperial persecutor as trying as the real thing must have been. These slips of girls defy " law and order " in the person of the Emperor Hadrian much as in our own day youthful suffragettes used to defy British magistrates. Probably this is in accordance with truth. Roswitha was separated from the days of the first Christians by a shorter space of time than that which separates us from her, and she based her narrative poem about the martyrdom of Saint Pelagius on an account given her by an eye-witness. While modern authors (with the exception of Mr. Bernard Shaw, whose Christian martyrs in *Androcles and the Lion* bear a resemblance to Roswitha's) love to dwell on the dignity of the early converts to Christianity, Roswitha conveys the impression that the dignity was mingled with impudence.

In *Callimachus, Abraham,* and *Paphnutius,* Roswitha sets out to describe the war between the flesh and the spirit, and the long penance which must be done by those who have allowed the flesh to triumph.   It is not enough for them to be converted and to realise their crime against the infinite beauty and goodness of God.   They are called on to take practical measures to cleanse themselves. *Callimachus* is the first of these plays, and by no means the best, although it timidly sounds a note of passion, rare, if it exists at all, in medieval literature.   Some commentators have laboured to establish a resemblance between *Callimachus* and *Romeo and Juliet*, and there are curious parallels.   In both you see a sepulchre, a woman's open grave, and the shroud lifted by the desperate hand of a lover.   In both two men come to this tragic scene, bowed down by grief, yet able to control it —in *Romeo and Juliet*, Capulet and Friar Lawrence, in *Callimachus,* the husband of the dead woman and the Apostle John.   It would be idle to strain the parallels too far.   They might not strike the attention at all if *Callimachus* did not possess a touch of the spirit of *Romeo and Juliet*.   It is this which makes the play seem to belong to a later period than the others, and gives it a different character.   The passionate language employed, the romance of the story, the colour of the earlier scenes are extraordinary when we remember that the play was written in the 10th century.   Haltingly, and apparently without any conscious intention, Roswitha describes the

kind of love of which Terence her model knew nothing
—that feverish desire absorbing the senses and the soul,
which leads to sin or madness or self-slaughter. As if
frightened by her own daring (or did the Abbess intervene,
as we guess she intervened in *Dulcitius*!), Roswitha spoils
the play as a play by a lengthy and tedious final scene
in which St. John appears to more advantage as a theo-
logian than as a man.

Abraham and *Paphnutius* show Roswitha at her best as
a dramatist. In both plays the scenes are well knit, the
characterization deft and sure, and the dialogue admirably
expressive. The opening scenes of *Abraham* reveal that
power to suggest character and situation without wordy
explanations which is essential in drama. We know at
once, although we are not told, that Mary, mere child as
she is, is not made of stern stuff, and that her vocation
is doubtful. Her replies to the two holy hermits are all
that they should be superficially, but through them penetrates a materialism antagonistic to their mystical exalta-
tion. Equally rich in the quality of suggestion is the
scene in the house of ill-fame which Abraham visits to
rescue his niece from her evil life. She does not recognize him at first, but melancholy seizes her at the supper
which it is her duty to enliven by her gaiety. There is
the beauty which never ages and appeals to all nations
in all times in the following scene, when the hermit,
throwing off his worldly disguise, shows his hair grown
white through vigils and fasts, and his tonsure, the badge

of his thorn-crowned Master, and in words more compassionate than upbraiding moves his lost child to contrition.   It is indeed amazing that so true and touching a scene, dealing with a subject which has led later dramatists into false sentiment, coarseness, or mere preaching, should have been written nearly a thousand years ago by an obscure nun in a convent in Lower Saxony.

Perhaps nothing in *Paphnutius* is on quite the same level of achievement, but a play is not made by a single scene, and *Paphnutius* as a whole is better than *Abraham* as a whole.   Few will question that it is Roswitha's masterpiece.   It is very creditable to her that, although the stories of the two plays are similar, she should have shown such variety in the treatment of them.   When we compare them we find hardly any repetition.   It is interesting to notice that it is not Mary, brought up to the religious life from which she lapses and to which she turns again, who becomes a saint, but Thais, whose life from childhood has been spent in " dangerous delights."   There is a spice of irony in the fact that the penitence of Thais, who had not had Mary's opportunities, is represented by the dramatist as being on a much higher spiritual plane.   With true insight Roswitha makes Paphnutius treat his penitent with far more severity than the hermit Abraham treats Mary.   Yet the angelic love of Paphnutius for Thais, thanks to the dramatist's power of suggestion, penetrates through his austerity, although he never manifests it until the moment when he is assured through the vision of Paul, St. Anthony's

disciple, that the repentance of the sinner has caused
that joy in heaven which exceeds all the joy that can
be given by the righteous. *Paphnutius* alone among
Roswitha's plays has stood the test of stage representation in modern times,* and come through it triumphantly,
although the miraculous swiftness of Thais's conversion
was considered most " unnatural " by the critics who
witnessed the performance.

Roswitha, it must be remembered, believed in miracles.
The average Englishman is sceptical.   As Mr. Chesterton
has pointed out, he will not swear to the possibility of a
thing he has not seen, although he is quite ready to swear
to the impossibility of a thing he has seen.   In the fore-
word which Mr. Chesterton wrote for the programme
of the first performance of *Paphnutius* he compared
Roswitha's treatment of the story of Thais's conversion
with Anatole France's in his well-known novel " Thais."
" This very strong and moving play (*Paphnutius*) was
written by a person about as different from the author of
' Thais ' as could be capable of wearing the human form,
a devout woman, vowed to a restricted life, and writing
in the light of a Latin that was gradually going out like a
shortening candle. . . . It is inevitable that such darkness
should breed dangerous and even savage things, and that

* Since this was written *Callimachus* (translation by
Arthur Waley) has been produced by the Art Theatre.
Paphnutius, in my translation, was produced by Miss
Edith Craig for the Pioneer Players at the Savoy Theatre
on June 4, 1914, Miss Ellen Terry appearing in the
part of the Abbess.

even religion should become almost as fierce as its enemies.
. . . This nun of the Dark Ages wrote without any of
that modern comfort and culture which ought, at the very
least, to make men kind.   When M. Anatole France
was the author of ' Silvestre Bonnard ' it did make him
kind.   But about Paphnutius and Thais, the harsh
ascetic of the hardest times of the 10th century is far
kinder than he.   In the ' Thais ' of the great French
romancer the whole point is that Thais repents but that
Paphnutius relapses.   The nun saves both souls.   Anatole
France loses one of them.   That is modern universalism."

I hope that the publication of these plays in the English
language will confirm Roswitha's right to a high place
in medieval literature, and a place also among the few
writers of plays which have more than a transitory interest.
Perhaps a certain predilection for medieval art is necessary
before we can love her wholeheartedly.   I do not
imagine that those who see no beauty in the primitive
art of Cimabue, Giotto, Sana di Pietro, or Lorenzetti
will admire the work of a primitive dramatist.   But
others who find sincere simplicity, as opposed to affected
simplicity, a charm in itself, will take Roswitha to their
hearts and will have no difficulty in recognizing her
merits.   In addition to the six plays I have translated
the five prefaces printed in Roswitha's complete works,
in the hope that the " strong voice of Gandersheim,"
speaking directly to the reader, may win a fresh interest
for the plays, and give some idea of the character and
attainments of the remarkable woman who wrote them.

CONTENTS

THE PREFACES OF ROSWITHA

PREFACE TO THE PLAYS OF HROTSWITHA, GERMAN RELIGIOUS AND VIRGIN OF THE SAXON RACE

THERE are many Catholics, and we cannot entirely acquit ourselves of the charge, who, attracted by the polished elegance of the style of pagan writers, prefer their works to the holy scriptures. There are others who, although they are deeply attached to the sacred writings and have no liking for most pagan productions, make an exception in favour of the works of Terence, and, fascinated by the charm of the manner, risk being corrupted by the wickedness of the matter. Wherefore I, the strong voice of Gandersheim, have not hesitated to imitate in my writings a poet whose works are so widely read, my object being to glorify, within the limits of my poor talent, the laudable chastity of Christian virgins in that self-same form of composition which has been used to describe the shameless acts of licentious women. One thing has all the same embarrassed me and often brought a blush to my cheek. It is that I have been compelled through the nature of this work to apply my mind and my pen to depicting the dreadful frenzy of those possessed by unlawful love, and the insidious sweetness of passion —things which should not even be named among us. Yet if from modesty I had refrained from treating these subjects I should not have been able to attain my object— to glorify the innocent to the best of my ability. For the more seductive the blandishments of lovers the more wonderful the divine succour and the greater the merit of those who resist, especially when it is fragile woman who is victorious and strong man who is routed with confusion.

I have no doubt that many will say that my poor work is much inferior to that of the author whom I have taken as my model, that it is on a much humbler scale, and indeed altogether different.

Well, I do not deny this. None can justly accuse me of wishing to place myself on a level with those who by the sublimity of their genius have so far outstripped me. No, I am not so arrogant as to compare myself even with the least among the scholars of the ancient world. I strive only, although my power is not equal to my desire, to use what talent I have for the glory of Him Who gave it me. Nor is my self-love so great that I would, to avoid criticism, abstain from proclaiming wherever possible the virtue of Christ working in His saints. If

this pious devotion gives satisfaction I shall rejoice ; it
it does not, either on account of my own worthlessness
or of the faults of my unpolished style, I shall still be glad
that I made the effort.

In the humbler works of my salad days I gathered up
my poor researches in heroic strophes, but here I have
sifted them into a series of dramatic scenes and avoided
through omission the pernicious voluptuousness of pagan
writers.

EPISTLE OF THE SAME TO CERTAIN LEARNED PATRONS OF THIS BOOK

To you, learned and virtuous men, who do not envy
the success of others, but on the contrary rejoice in it as
becomes the truly great, Hrotswitha, poor humble sinner,
sends wishes for your health in this life and your joy in
eternity.

I cannot praise you enough for your humility, or pay
an adequate tribute to your kindness and affection.   To
think that you, who have been nurtured in the most pro-
found philosophical studies and have attained knowledge
in perfection, should have deigned to approve the humble
work of an obscure woman !   You have, however, not
praised me but the Giver of the grace which works in me,
by sending me your paternal congratulations and admitting
that I possess some little knowledge of those arts the
subtleties of which exceed the grasp of my woman's

mind.   Until I showed my work to you I had not dared
to let anyone see it except my intimate companions.
I came near abandoning this form of writing altogether,
for if there were few to whom I could submit my compositions at all there were fewer still who could point
out what needed correction and encourage me to go on.
But now, reassured by your verdict (is it not said that
the testimony of three witnesses is "equivalent to the
truth"?), I feel that I have enough confidence to apply
myself to writing, if God grants me the power, and that
I need not fear the criticism of the learned whoever they
may be.   Still, I am torn by conflicting feelings.   I
rejoice from the depths of my soul that the God through
Whose grace alone I am what I am should be praised
in me, but I am afraid of being thought greater than
I am.   I know that it is as wrong to deny a divine gift
as to pretend falsely that we have received it.   So I will
not deny that through the grace of the Creator I have
acquired some knowledge of the arts.   He has given me
the ability to learn—I am a teachable creature—yet of
myself I should know nothing.   He has given me a
perspicacious mind, but one that lies fallow and idle
when it is not cultivated.   That my natural gifts might
not be made void by negligence I have been at pains,
whenever I have been able to pick up some threads and
scraps torn from the old mantle of philosophy, to weave
them into the stuff of my own book, in the hope that
my lowly ignorant effort may gain more acceptance

through the introduction of something of a nobler strain, and that the Creator of genius may be the more honoured since it is generally believed that a woman's intelligence is slower. Such has been my motive in writing, the sole reason for the sweat and fatigue which my labours have cost me. At least I do not pretend to have knowledge where I am ignorant. On the contrary, my best claim to indulgence is that I know how much I do not know.

Impelled by your kindly interest and your express wish I come, bowing low like a reed, to submit this little work to your judgment. I wrote it indeed with that idea in my mind, although doubt as to its merits has made me withhold it until now. I hope you will revise it with the same careful attention that you would give to a work of your own, and that when you have succeeded in bringing it up to the proper standard you will return it to me, that I may learn what are its worst faults.

ROSWITHA'S PREFACE TO HER POETICAL WORKS

(The Life Story of the Blessed Virgin, The Fall and Conversion of Theophilus, The Martyrdom of Saint Agnes, Poems concerning the First Cenobites at Gandersheim, The Acts of Otho I, etc., etc.)

I offer this little book, which has not much to recommend it in the way of beauty, although it has been compiled with a good deal of care, for the criticism of all those learned people who do not take pleasure in a writer's faults but are anxious to amend them. I am well aware that in my first works I made many mistakes not only in prosody but in literary composition, and there must be much to criticise in this book. By acknowledging my shortcomings beforehand I hope I am entitled to ready indulgence as well as to careful correction of my mistakes. To the objection that may be raised that I have borrowed parts of this work from authorities which some condemn as apocryphal, I would answer that I have erred through ignorance, not through presumption. When I started, timidly enough, on the work of composition I did not know that the authenticity of my material had been questioned. On discovering this to be the case I decided not to discard it, because it often happens that what is reputed false turns out to be true. In these circumstances I shall need as much assistance in defending this little work as in improving it. It must be remembered that when I began it I was far from possessing the necessary qualifications, being young both in years and learning. Up to the present I have not submitted the work to any experts much as I needed their advice, for fear that the roughness of the style would make them discourage me to such an extent that I might give up writing altogether. Unknown to all round me, I have toiled in secret, often destroying what seemed to me to be ill written, and rewriting it. I have tried to the best of my ability to improvise on phrases collected from sacred writings in the precincts of our convent at Gandersheim. I was trained first by our most learned and gentle novice-mistress Rikkarda and others. Later, I owed much to the kind favour and encouragement of a royal personage, Gerberga, under whose abbatial rule I am now living. She, though younger in years than I, was, as might be expected of the niece of an Emperor, far older in learning, and she had the kindness to make me familiar with the works of some of those authors in whose writings she had been instructed by learned men. Although prosody may seem a hard and difficult art for a woman to master, I, without any assistance but that given by the merciful grace of Heaven (in which I have trusted, rather than in my own strength), have attempted in this book to sing in dactyls. I was eager that the talent given me by Heaven should not grow rusty from neglect, and remain silent in my heart from apathy, but under the hammer of assiduous devotion should sound a chord of divine praise. If I have achieved nothing else, this alone should make my work of some value. Wherefore, reader, whosoever you may be, I beg you, if you think it right before God, to help me by not sparing censure of such pages as are poor and lack the skill of a master. If, on the contrary, you find some that stand the test of criticism, give the credit to God, ascribing all defects to my shortcomings. Do this in an indulgent rather than in a censorious spirit, for the critic forfeits the right to be severe when the writer acknowledges defects with humility.

TO GERBERG

Illustrious Abbess, venerated no less for uprightness and honesty than for the high distinction of a royal and noble race, Roswitha of Gandersheim, the last of the least of those fighting under your ladyship's rule, desires to give you all that a servant owes her mistress.

O my Lady, bright with the varied jewels of spiritual wisdom, your maternal kindness will not let you hesitate to read what, as you know, was written at your command ! It was you who gave me the task of chronicling in verse the deeds of the Emperor, and you know that it was impossible to collect them together from hearsay. You can imagine the difficulties which my ignorance put in my way while I was toiling over this work. There were things of which I could not find any written record, nor could I elicit information by word of mouth which seemed sufficiently reliable. I was like a person in a strange land wandering without a guide through a forest where the path is concealed by dense snow. In vain he tries to follow the directions of those who have shown the way. He wanders from the path, now by chance strikes it again, until at last, penetrating the thickness of the wood, he reaches a place where he may take a long-desired rest, and sitting down there, does not proceed further until someone overtakes him, or he discovers the footprints of one who has gone before. Even so have I, obeying the command to undertake a complete chronicle of great deeds, gone on my way, trembling, hesitating, and vacillating, so great was the difficulty of finding a path in the forest of these royal achievements.

And now, worn out by the journey, I am holding my peace and resting in a suitable place. I do not propose to go further without better guidance. If I could be inspired by the eloquent words of learned folk (either already set down or to be set down in the future) I might perhaps find a means of glozing my uncouth workmanship. At present I am defenceless at every point, because I am not supported by any authority. I also fear I shall be accused of temerity in presuming to describe in my humble uncultured way matters which ought to be set forth with all the ceremony of great learning. Yet if my work is examined by those who know how to weigh things fairly, I shall be more easily pardoned on account of my sex and my inferior knowledge, especially as I did not undertake it of my own will but at your command. Why should I fear the judgment of others, since if there are mistakes I should fall only under your censure, and why should I not escape reproof seeing that I was anxious to keep silence ? I should deserve blame if I sought to withhold my work. In any case I leave the decision to you and your friend, Archbishop William, to whom you have thought fit to show these unpolished lines.

ROSWITHA'S PREFACE TO THE COMPLETE WORKS

I FOUND all the material I have used in this book in various ancient works by authors of reputation, with the exception of the story of the martyrdom of St. Pelagius, which has been told here in verse. The details of this were supplied to me by an inhabitant of the town where the Saint was put to death. This truthful stranger assured me that he had not only seen Pelagius, whom he described as the most beautiful of men, face to face, but had been a witness of his end. If anything has crept into my other compositions, the accuracy of which can be challenged, it is not my fault, unless it be a fault to have reproduced the statements of unreliable authorities.

GALLICANUS

ARGUMENT

THE conversion of Gallicanus, Commander-in-Chief. On the eve of his departure for a campaign against the Scythians, Gallicanus is betrothed to the Emperor Constantine's daughter, Constance, a consecrated virgin.

When threatened with defeat in battle, Gallicanus is converted by John and Paul, Grand Almoners to Constance. He is immediately baptized and takes a vow of celibacy.

Later he is exiled by order of Julian the Apostate, and receives the crown of martyrdom. John and Paul are put to death by the same prince and buried secretly in their own house. Not long after, the son of their executioner becomes possessed by a devil. He is cured after confessing the crime committed by his father. He bears witness to the merits of the martyrs, and is baptized, together with his father.

CHARACTERS IN PART I

THE EMPEROR CONSTANTINE.
GALLICANUS.
CONSTANCE (*Daughter of Constantine*).
ARTEMIA ⎱
ATTICA ⎰ (*Daughters of Gallicanus*).
JOHN ⎫
  and ⎬ (*Grand Almoners to Constance*).
PAUL ⎭
LORDS OF THE COURT.
BRADAN (*King of the Scythians*).
TRIBUNES.
ROMAN SOLDIERS.
SCYTHIAN SOLDIERS.
HELENA (*Mother of Constantine*).

CHARACTERS IN PART II

JULIAN (*The Apostate*).
GALLICANUS.
TERENTIANUS.
JOHN.
PAUL.
CONSULS.
CHRISTIANS.
SOLDIERS.

GALLICANUS

SCENE I

CONSTANTINE. Gallicanus, this tries my patience. You have delayed the offensive against the Scythians too long. The only nation which boldly resists our power and refuses to make peace with Rome! You know well enough that you were chosen because of your energy in your country's service.

GALLICANUS. Most noble Constantine, I have served you hand and foot, ungrudgingly, devotedly, and have always striven to repay your trust in me with deeds. I have never shirked any task.

CONSTANTINE. Is there any need to remind me? As if your great services were not always in mind! I spoke, not to reproach you, but to urge you to act quickly.

GALLICANUS. I will set out at once.

CONSTANTINE. I am rejoiced to hear it.

GALLICANUS. I am ready to obey your orders if it costs me my life.

CONSTANTINE. Your zeal pleases me. I appreciate your devotion.

GALLICANUS. As both are immense should they not be rewarded on the same scale ?

CONSTANTINE. That is only fair.

GALLICANUS. It is easier for a man to undertake a difficult enterprise when he is sustained by the knowledge that his reward is sure.

CONSTANTINE. Naturally.

GALLICANUS. I beg you then to promise me now my prize for this dangerous undertaking. In hard and strenuous fighting, when it seems as if I must be defeated, the thought of this reward will give me new strength.

CONSTANTINE. The reward deemed by the Senate the most glorious a man can desire has never been withheld from you, and never shall be. You enjoy the freedom of my court, and the highest honour among those who surround me.

GALLICANUS. I know, but I am not thinking of that.

CONSTANTINE. If you have other ambitions, you must tell me.

GALLICANUS. I have.

CONSTANTINE. What are they ?

GALLICANUS. Dare I tell you ?

CONSTANTINE. Of course !

GALLICANUS. You will be angry.

CONSTANTINE. Not at all !

GALLICANUS. You are sure ?

CONSTANTINE. Quite sure.

GALLICANUS. We shall see. I say you will be indignant.

CONSTANTINE. Your fears are groundless. Come! Speak!

GALLICANUS. Since you command me, I will. I love Constance. I love your daughter.

CONSTANTINE. That is well. You do right to love the daughter of your sovereign. Your love honours her.

GALLICANUS. You say this to cut me short.

CONSTANTINE. Not so.

GALLICANUS. I wish to marry her. Will you give your consent?

CONSTANTINE. He asks no small thing, my lords. This is an honour of which none of you have ever dreamed.

GALLICANUS. Alas! I foresaw this. He scorns me. (*To the Lords*) Intercede for me, I implore you.

THE LORDS. Most illustrious Emperor, we beg you to be generous. Remember his services, and do not turn a deaf ear to his request.

CONSTANTINE. I have not done so, but it is my duty first to make sure that my daughter consents.

THE LORDS. That is only reasonable.

CONSTANTINE. I will go to her, and, if such is your wish, Gallicanus, I will lay the project before her.

GALLICANUS. It is my wish.

SCENE II

CONSTANCE. Our Lord the Emperor approaches. He looks strangely grave and sad. What can it mean?

CONSTANTINE. Constance, my child, come nearer. I wish to speak to you.

CONSTANCE. I am here, my lord. Command me.

CONSTANTINE. I am in great distress of mind. My heart is heavy.

CONSTANCE. As you came in I saw that you were sad, and without knowing the reason I was troubled.

CONSTANTINE. It is on your account.

CONSTANCE. On my account?

CONSTANTINE. Yes.

CONSTANCE. You frighten me. What is it, my lord?

CONSTANTINE. The fear of grieving you ties my tongue.

CONSTANCE. You will grieve me more by keeping silence.

CONSTANTINE. Gallicanus, my General, whose victories have won him the first place among the princes of my realm—Gallicanus, whose sword is necessary for the defence of the Empire—Gallicanus——

CONSTANCE. What of him?

CONSTANTINE. He wants to make you his wife.

CONSTANCE. Me?

CONSTANTINE. Yes.

CONSTANCE. I would rather die.

CONSTANTINE. I knew that would be your answer.

CONSTANCE. It cannot surprise you, as it was with your consent and approval that I consecrated myself to God.

CONSTANTINE. I have not forgotten.

CONSTANCE. I will keep my vow inviolate. Nothing can ever force me to break it.

CONSTANTINE. I know you are right, and the greater my difficulty. For if, as is my duty as your father, I permit you to be faithful to your vow, as a sovereign I shall suffer for it. Yet were I to oppose your resolution—which God forbid!—I should deserve eternal punishment.

CONSTANCE. If I despaired of divine help I should be more wretched than you.

CONSTANTINE. That is true.

CONSTANCE. But a heart which trusts in God's goodness is armed against sorrow.

CONSTANTINE. You speak well, my Constance.

CONSTANCE. My lord, if you will deign to listen to my advice, I can show you how to escape this double danger.

CONSTANTINE. Oh, that you could!

CONSTANCE. You must pretend that you are willing to grant Gallicanus what he asks when the war has been won. Make him believe that I agree. Persuade him to leave with me during his absence at the war his two daughters, Attica and Artemia, as pledges of the bond of love which is to unite us. Tell him that in return I will send with him on his expedition my two Almoners, John and Paul.

CONSTANTINE. And if he should return victorious? What then?

CONSTANCE. We must pray the Father of us all that he will change his mind.

CONSTANTINE. My daughter, my daughter! Your sweet words have softened the harshness of your father's grief! Henceforth I will not give way to anxiety.

CONSTANCE. There is no need.

CONSTANTINE. I will return to Gallicanus and satisfy him with this promise.

CONSTANCE. Go in peace, my lord.

SCENE III

GALLICANUS. O princes, I die of impatience to learn what has come of this long conference between our august sovereign and his daughter.

THE LORDS. He promised to plead your cause.

GALLICANUS. Oh, that his arguments may prevail!

THE LORDS. Maybe they will.

GALLICANUS. Peace! Silence all of you! The Emperor comes. His face is not anxious as when he left us, but serene and glad.

THE LORDS. A good omen!

GALLICANUS. It is said that the face is the mirror of the soul. If this be true, the calm joy in his reflects a kindly mood.

THE LORDS. We trust so.

SCENE IV

CONSTANTINE. Gallicanus !

GALLICANUS. What did he say ?

THE LORDS. Forward, forward. He is asking for you

GALLICANUS. Now the good gods help me !

CONSTANTINE. Gallicanus, set out for the war with an easy mind. On your return you shall receive the reward you covet.

GALLICANUS. This is not a jest ?

CONSTANTINE. How can you ask ?

GALLICANUS. I should be happy indeed if I could know one thing.

CONSTANTINE. What may that be ?

GALLICANUS. Her answer.

CONSTANTINE. My daughter's answer ?

GALLICANUS. Yes. What did she say ?

CONSTANTINE. It is unreasonable to expect a young maid to answer in so many words. Events will prove that she consents.

GALLICANUS. If I could be assured of that, I should trouble little about the manner of her answer.

CONSTANTINE. You want proof ?

GALLICANUS. I hunger for it.

CONSTANTINE. Then listen. She has given orders that her Almoners, John and Paul, shall stay with you until the day of your nuptials.

GALLICANUS. And her reason ?

CONSTANTINE. That by constant intercourse with them you may learn to know how she lives—her habits and her tastes.

GALLICANUS. An excellent plan, and one that pleases me beyond measure.

CONSTANTINE. She would like you in return to allow your two young daughters to live with her for the same period. She thinks she can learn from them how to please you.

GALLICANUS. Oh, joy, joy ! All things are falling out as I wished.

CONSTANTINE. Send for your daughters without delay.

GALLICANUS. Are my soldiers still there ? Come, fellows, hasten ! Run to my daughters and bring them to their sovereign's presence.

SCENE V

SOLDIERS. Most noble Constance, the illustrious daughters of Gallicanus are here. They are beautiful, wise and virtuous, and in every way worthy of your friendship.

CONSTANCE. They are welcome. (*They are intro-*

duced with ceremony.) * O Christ, lover of virginity and fount of chastity! Thou Who through the intercession of Thy holy martyr Agnes hast preserved my body from stain and my mind from pagan errors! Thou Who hast shown me as an example Thy Mother's virgin bed where Thou didst manifest Thyself true God! Thou Who before time began wast born of God the Father, and in the fullness of time wast born again true man, of a mother's womb — I implore Thee, true Wisdom, co-eternal with the Father, the Creator, Upholder and Governor of the Universe, to grant my prayer! May Gallicanus, who seeks to gain the love which I can give only to Thee, be turned from his unlawful purpose. Take his daughters to Thyself, and pour the sweetness of Thy love into their hearts that they may despise all carnal bonds, and be admitted to the blessed company of virgins who are consecrated to Thee!

ARTEMIA. Hail, most noble Constance! Imperial highness, hail!

CONSTANCE. Greeting, my sisters, Artemia and Attica. Stand up, stand up! No, do not kneel. Salute me rather with a loving kiss.

ARTEMIA. We come joyfully to offer you our homage, lady. We are ready to serve you with our whole hearts, and we seek no reward but your love.

---

* Celtes prints this as part of the text; Magnin as a direction, on the ground that it is *introducuntur,* not *introducautur* in the MS.

CONSTANCE. We have one Lord Who is in heaven. He alone should be served like that. We owe Him a love and fidelity which must be shown not only with whole hearts but with whole bodies. That is if we would enter His kingdom with the virgin's palm.

ARTEMIA. We do not question this. You will find us eager to obey you in all things, but never so eager as when you exhort us to confess our faith and keep our vow of purity.

CONSTANCE. That is a good answer, and one worthy of a noble mind. I see that through divine grace you already have the faith.

ARTEMIA. How could we poor idolators have any good thought if light had not been given us from above?

CONSTANCE. The strength of your faith makes me hope that Gallicanus too will believe some day.

ARTEMIA. He has only to be taught. Then he must believe.

CONSTANCE. Send for John and Paul.

SCENE VI

JOHN. You sent for us, Highness. We are here.

CONSTANCE. Go at once to Gallicanus and attach yourselves to his person. Instruct him little by little in the mysteries of our faith. Perhaps God means to make us the instruments of winning him to His service.

PAUL. God give us success! We shall do all we can.

SCENE VII

GALLICANUS. You are welcome, John—and you, Paul. I have awaited your coming with impatience.

JOHN. As soon as we received our lady's commands we hastened at once to put ourselves at your service.

GALLICANUS. Your offer to serve me gives me a pleasure that nothing else could give.

PAUL. That is natural, for, as the saying goes, "The friends of our friends are our friends."

GALLICANUS. A true saying.

JOHN. The love our lady bears you assures us of your goodwill.

GALLICANUS. You can rely on it. Come, tribunes and centurions, assemble the troops. Soldiers in my command, I present to you John and Paul, for whose arrival our departure has been delayed.

TRIBUNES. Lead us on. (*The tribunes gather round Gallicanus.*) *

GALLICANUS. We must first go to the Capitol, and visit the temples to propitiate the gods with the customary sacrifices. That is the way to obtain success for our arms.

TRIBUNES. That is certain.

JOHN. Let us withdraw for a time.

PAUL. We cannot do otherwise.

* Another " stage direction " omitted by Celtes.

SCENE VIII

JOHN. The General is leaving the temple. Let us mount our horses and ride to meet him.

PAUL. This moment.

GALLICANUS. I noticed you were not with us. Where have you been ?

JOHN. We were seeing to our baggage. We have sent it on ahead that we may ride with you unencumbered.

GALLICANUS. Well planned !

SCENE IX

GALLICANUS. By Jupiter, tribunes, I see the legions of an immense army advancing ! The diversity of their arms is enough to make the stoutest heart tremble.

TRIBUNES. By Hercules, the enemy !

GALLICANUS. Let us resist with courage, and show them we are men !

TRIBUNES. It is useless to attempt resistance to such a host.

GALLICANUS. What, then, do you propose ?

TRIBUNES. Surrender.

GALLICANUS. Apollo forbid !

TRIBUNES. By Pollux, we must surrender ! See, we are surrounded on every side—we are being mown down—we perish !

GALLICANUS. Ye gods ! What will happen if the tribunes refuse to obey me, and surrender ?

JOHN. Promise you will become a Christian, and you will conquer.

GALLICANUS. I swear ! And I will keep my vow.

ONE OF THE ENEMY. Woe to us, King Bradan ! Fortune, who but now promised us victory, was mocking us. Our men are weakening, their strength is exhausted —they have lost heart and are giving up the struggle.

BRADAN. I am uncertain what to do. A strange faint-heartedness has seized me also. There is but one course— we must surrender.

THE ENEMY. There is nothing else to do.

BRADAN. Gallicanus, do not destroy us ! Be merci-ful ! Spare our lives and do with us what you will.

GALLICANUS. Have no fear. There is no need to tremble. Give me hostages, acknowledge yourselves tributaries of the Emperor, and you shall live happy under a Roman peace.

BRADAN. You have only to name the number and rank of the hostages, and the tribute to be exacted.

GALLICANUS. Soldiers, lay down arms. Slay no one, wound no one, but embrace as friends these men whom you had to fight as enemies of the Empire.

JOHN. How much more powerful is one fervent prayer than all the pride of man !

GALLICANUS. That is true indeed.

PAUL. What mighty succour God in His mercy sends to those who humbly trust in Him !

GALLICANUS. I have had good proof of it.

JOHN. But the promise made when the storm was raging must be kept now it is calm.

GALLICANUS. I agree. It is my wish to be baptized as soon as possible, and to devote the rest of my life to the service of God.

PAUL. You are right.

SCENE X

GALLICANUS. Look ! That vast crowd of citizens has gathered to see our entry into Rome ! See how they flock to acclaim us, bearing according to custom the symbols of victory !

JOHN. It is only natural.

GALLICANUS. Yet the glorious victory was not won by my valour nor by the help of their gods.

JOHN. No, assuredly ; the glory belongs to the one true God.

GALLICANUS. That being so, we must pass the temples without going in.

JOHN. A wise decision.

GALLICANUS. And instead make a humble confession of faith in the Church of the Apostles.

PAUL. O happy man ! And most happy thought ! In this you show yourself a true Christian.

SCENE XI

CONSTANTINE. I am greatly astonished, soldiers, that Gallicanus should be so long in presenting himself before his sovereign.

SOLDIERS. The moment he arrived in Rome he went to the Church of Saint Peter, and, prostrating himself on the ground, gave thanks to the Almighty for giving him the victory.

CONSTANTINE. Gallicanus?

SOLDIERS. It is true.

CONSTANTINE. Impossible!

SOLDIERS. Here he comes. You can ask him yourself.

SCENE XII

CONSTANTINE. Welcome, Gallicanus! I have awaited your arrival with impatience. I long to hear from your own lips how the battle went and how it ended.

GALLICANUS. I will tell you the whole story.

CONSTANTINE. Wait a moment, for even the battle is of small importance compared with the one thing which I want most to hear.

GALLICANUS. What may that be?

CONSTANTINE. On your departure for the war you visited the temple of the gods; on your return you went to the Church of the Apostles. Why?

GALLICANUS. You ask that?

CONSTANTINE. Have I not told you, man, that I wish to know above all things !

GALLICANUS. I will explain.

CONSTANTINE. Proceed, I beg you.

GALLICANUS. Most Sacred Emperor, I confess I visited the temples on my departure, as you have said, and humbly sought the help of gods and demons.

CONSTANTINE. According to the old Roman custom.

GALLICANUS. To my thinking, a bad custom.

CONSTANTINE. I am of the same mind.

GALLICANUS. Then the tribunes arrived with their legions and we began our march.

CONSTANTINE. You set out from Rome with great pomp.

GALLICANUS. We pushed on, met the enemy, engaged them, and were defeated.

CONSTANTINE. Romans defeated !

GALLICANUS. Routed.

CONSTANTINE. When was such a disaster ever known in our history !

GALLICANUS. Once again I offered those hideous sacrifices, but what god came to my help ? The fury of the enemy redoubled, and great numbers of my men were slain.

CONSTANTINE. I am amazed.

GALLICANUS. It was then that the tribunes, disregarding my orders, began to surrender.

CONSTANTINE. To the enemy ?

GALLICANUS. To the enemy.

CONSTANTINE. And what did you do ?

GALLICANUS. What could I do but take to flight ?

CONSTANTINE. Impossible !

GALLICANUS. It is true.

CONSTANTINE. What anguish for a man of your courage !

GALLICANUS. The sharpest.

CONSTANTINE. And how did you escape ?

GALLICANUS. My faithful companions, John and Paul, advised me to make a vow to the Creator.

CONSTANTINE. Good advice.

GALLICANUS. I found it so. Hardly had I opened my lips to make the vow than I received help from heaven.

CONSTANTINE. How ?

GALLICANUS. A young man of immense stature appeared before me carrying a cross on his shoulder. He bade me follow him sword in hand.

CONSTANTINE. This young man, whoever he was, was sent from heaven.

GALLICANUS. So it proved. At the same moment I saw at my side some soldiers whose faces were strange to me. They promised me their help.

CONSTANTINE. The host of Heaven !

GALLICANUS. I am sure of it. Following in the steps of my guide, I advanced fearlessly into the midst of the enemy until I came face to face with their King, by name Bradan. Suddenly overcome by the strangest terror he threw himself at my feet, surrendered with his whole army, and promised to pay tribute in perpetuity to the ruler of the Roman world.

CONSTANTINE. Now praise be to Him Who gave us this victory. Those who put their trust in Him will never be confounded.

GALLICANUS. My experience witnesses to it.

CONSTANTINE. And now I should like to know what became of the treacherous tribunes ?

GALLICANUS. They hastened to implore my forgiveness.

CONSTANTINE. And you showed them mercy ?

GALLICANUS. I show mercy to men who had abandoned me in the hour of peril and surrendered to the enemy against my orders ! No, assuredly !

CONSTANTINE. What did you do ?

GALLICANUS. I offered to pardon them on one condition.

CONSTANTINE. What condition ?

GALLICANUS. I told them that those who consented to become Christians would be allowed to retain their rank, and might even receive fresh honours, but that those who refused would not be pardoned, and would be degraded.

CONSTANTINE. A fair proposition, and honourable to the leader who made it.

GALLICANUS. For my own part, purified in the waters of baptism, I have surrendered myself completely to the will of God. I am ready to renounce even your daughter, whom I love more than anything in the world. I wish to abstain from marriage that I may devote myself wholly to the service of the Virgin's Son.

CONSTANTINE. Come near, nearer yet, and let me fold you in my arms ! Now, Gallicanus, the time has come for me to tell you what up to now I have been obliged to keep secret.

GALLICANUS. What is it ?

CONSTANTINE. My daughter, and your own two also, have chosen the same holy path which you yourself wish to follow.

GALLICANUS. I rejoice to hear it.

CONSTANTINE. Their desire to keep their vow of virginity is so ardent that neither entreaties nor threats can alter their resolution.

GALLICANUS. God help them to persevere !

CONSTANTINE. Come, let us go to their apartments.

GALLICANUS. Lead on. I will follow.

CONSTANTINE. They are coming here. Look, they hasten to greet us, and my glorious mother, noble Helena, is with them. They all weep for joy.

SCENE XIII

GALLICANUS. Be at peace, most holy virgins. Persevere in the fear of God, and preserve untouched the treasure of your virginity. Then you will be worthy of the embraces of the eternal King.

CONSTANCE. We shall keep our vows with more joy now we know that you are on our side.

GALLICANUS. Have no fear that I shall put any obstacle in your way. Far from it! I consent gladly, and desire nothing better than to see you fulfil your vow, my Constance, you, for whom I was eager to risk life itself.

CONSTANCE. I see the hand of the Most High in this change in you.

GALLICANUS. If I had not changed, and for the better, I could never have consented to renounce you.

CONSTANCE. The Lover of virginal purity and the Author of all good resolutions made you renounce me because He had already claimed me for His own. May He Who has separated us in the body on earth unite us in the joys of eternity.

GALLICANUS. So be it! So be it!

CONSTANTINE. And now, since we are united in the bond of Christ's love, you shall live with us in our palace, and be treated with as much honour as though you were our own son.

GALLICANUS. What temptation is to be feared more than the lust of the eyes?

CONSTANTINE. None, I know.

GALLICANUS. Then is it right that I should see her too often? As you know, I love her more than my own kin, more than my life, more than my soul!

CONSTANTINE. You must do what you think best.

GALLICANUS. Thanks to our Lord Christ and to my labours, your army was never so strong as now. Give me leave, then, to transfer my service to that Emperor through Whose power I have returned victorious, and to Whom I owe any success I have won in life.

CONSTANTINE. To Him be praise and glory. All creatures should serve Him.

GALLICANUS. Above all those whom He has generously helped in time of need.

CONSTANTINE. That is true.

GALLICANUS. I am giving to my daughters the portion of my property which is theirs by right. Another I am devoting to the support of pilgrims. With the remainder I propose to enrich my slaves—whom I have freed—and to relieve the poor.

CONSTANTINE. You are disposing of your wealth wisely, and you will be rewarded.

GALLICANUS. As for me, I long to go to Ostia and become the disciple of the holy man, Hilarion. In his brotherhood I hope to spend the rest of my life praising God and helping the poor.

CONSTANTINE. May the Divine Being to Whom all things are possible bring your plans to a happy issue! May you always do the will of Him Who lives and reigns in the Unity of the Trinity, and at last attain eternal joy!

GALLICANUS. Amen.

GALLICANUS

PART II.—SCENE I

JULIAN. The cause of the unrest in our Empire is clear enough. These Christians enjoy too much liberty. Their claim that they obey laws made in the time of Constantine is false.

CONSULS. It would be a disgrace to tolerate it.

JULIAN. I do not intend to tolerate it.

CONSULS. Those words are worthy of you.

JULIAN. Soldiers, arm yourselves and strip the Christians of all they possess. Remind them of these words of their Christ :—" He who does not renounce all that he possesses for my sake cannot be my disciple."

SOLDIERS. We will carry out your orders instantly.

SCENE II

CONSULS. The soldiers have returned.

JULIAN. Is all well ?

SOLDIERS. Well indeed.

JULIAN. Why have you returned so soon ?

SOLDIERS. We will tell you. We had planned to seize Gallicanus's castle and occupy it in your name. But no sooner did one of us set foot on the threshold than he was straightway stricken with leprosy or madness.

JULIAN. Return and force Gallicanus to quit the realm or sacrifice to the gods.

SCENE III

GALLICANUS. Do not waste your breath, fellows. Your advice is useless. I hold all that exists beneath the sun as nothing compared with eternal life. Banished for Christ's sake, I shall retire to Alexandria, where I hope to win the martyr's crown.

SCENE IV

SOLDIERS. Gallicanus, exiled by your orders, fled to Alexandria. He was arrested in that city by the Governor, Ratianus, and has perished by the sword.

JULIAN. That is well.

SOLDIERS. But John and Paul still defy you.

JULIAN. What are they doing?

SOLDIERS. Travelling up and down the country giving away the fortune Constance left them.

JULIAN. Bring them before me.

SOLDIERS. They are here.

SCENE V

JULIAN. John and Paul, from the cradle you have been attached to the Emperor's household. You served my predecessor.

JOHN. That is so.

JULIAN. Then what could be more fitting than that you should serve me also in this palace where you were brought up ?

PAUL. We will not serve you.

JULIAN. You refuse ?

JOHN. We have said it.

JULIAN. Do you deny that I am Augustus ?

PAUL. No, but we say you are Augustus with a difference.

JULIAN. How do I differ from my predecessors ?

JOHN. In your religion and your virtue.

JULIAN. What do you mean ?

PAUL. We mean that those most famous and glorious princes, Constantine, Constantius and Constance, whom we served, were very Christian rulers who were zealous in the service of God.

JULIAN. I know, but in this I do not choose to follow their example.

PAUL. You follow worse examples. They frequented the churches and, laying their diadems on the ground, adored Jesus Christ on their knees.

JULIAN. And you think that I should imitate them ?

JOHN. You are not made of the same stuff.

PAUL. By doing homage to the Creator they elevated the Imperial dignity—yes, they transfigured it with the splendour of their virtue and their holy lives. So they deserved the success which crowned their enterprises.

JULIAN. As I do.

JOHN. In a very different way, for the divine grace was with them.

JULIAN. Absurd! Once I too was fool enough to believe in these meaningless practices. I was a priest of your Church.

JOHN. Do you hear, Paul? How do you like this priest?

PAUL. Very well—as the devil's chaplain.

JULIAN. But when I found that there was nothing to be gained from it, I turned to the worship of the true Roman gods, thanks to whom I have been raised to the highest pinnacle of power.

JOHN. You cut us short with this boast to avoid hearing the righteous praised.

JULIAN. What is it to me?

PAUL. Nothing; but we would add something which does concern you. When the world was no longer worthy of those princes, they were summoned to the choir of angels, and this unhappy realm fell under your power.

JULIAN. Why unhappy?

JOHN. Because of the character of its ruler.

PAUL. Have you not renounced the true religion and adopted the superstitions of idolatry ?   Because of this we have shunned you and your court.

JULIAN. You show yourselves greatly wanting in the respect due to me, yet I am ready to pardon your presumption and raise you to the highest office in my palace.

JOHN. You waste your breath, apostate ! We shall yield neither to blandishments nor threats.

JULIAN. I will give you ten days' grace, in the hope that you will come to your senses and repent. If you do, you will regain our Imperial favour. If not, I shall do what I have to do. You shall not make a mock of me.

PAUL. What you have to do, do now, for you can never make us return either to your court, your service, or your gods.

JULIAN. You are dismissed. Leave me, but heed my warning.

JOHN. We willingly accept the respite you have granted us, but only that we may spend the time consecrating all our faculties to heaven, and commending ourselves to God in prayer and fasting.

PAUL. This is all we have to do now.

SCENE VI

JULIAN. Go, Terentianus. Take with you a few trusted soldiers and compel John and Paul to sacrifice to

Jupiter. If they persist in their refusal, let them be put to death, not publicly, but with the greatest possible secrecy, since they once held office in this palace.

SCENE VII

TERENTIANUS. Paul and John, the Emperor Julian, my master, of his clemency sends you this gold statue of Jupiter, and commands you to burn incense before it. Refuse, and you will be put to death.

JOHN. Since Julian is your master, live at peace with him, and enjoy his favour. But we have no master except our Lord Jesus Christ, for Whose love we ardently desire to die that we may the more quickly taste the joys of eternity.

TERENTIANUS. Soldiers, why do you delay? Draw your swords and strike these traitors to the gods and to their Emperor. When they have breathed their last bury them secretly in this house and remove every trace of blood.

SOLDIERS. And if questions are asked, what are we to say?

TERENTIANUS. Say they have been banished.

JOHN. To Thee, O Christ, Who reigneth with the Father and the Holy Ghost, one God, we raise our voices in this dreadful hour! In death as in life we praise Thee.

PAUL. O Christ, receive our souls, which for Thy sake are being driven from this dwelling of clay!

SCENE VIII

TERENTIANUS. Christians, Christians, what ails my son ?

CHRISTIANS. He grinds his teeth, foams at the mouth, and rolls his eyes like a madman. He is sure possessed by a devil.

TERENTIANUS. Woe to his father ! Where was he stricken ?

CHRISTIANS. Before the tomb of the martyrs John and Paul. He writhes on the ground, and cries out that they are the cause of his torments.

TERENTIANUS. Mine the fault ! Mine the crime ! It was at my command that the wretched boy laid his impious hands on those holy martyrs.

CHRISTIANS. Since you were the partner of his guilt, it is right that you should share his sufferings.

TERENTIANUS. I did but obey the wicked commands of my master, the Emperor Julian.

CHRISTIANS. He himself has been struck down by the divine wrath.

TERENTIANUS. I know, and am the more terrified. I see that no enemy of those servants of God can escape punishment.

CHRISTIANS. You are right there.

TERENTIANUS. What if in expiation of my crime I threw myself on my knees before the holy tombs ?

CHRISTIANS. You would win pardon if you were first cleansed by baptism.

SCENE IX

TERENTIANUS. Glorious witnesses of Christ, John and Paul, follow the example and commandment of your Master, and pray for your persecutors. Have compassion on the anguish of a father who fears to lose his child! Have pity on the sufferings of the son! Succour us both, and grant that, purified in the waters of baptism, we may persevere in the faith.

CHRISTIANS. Dry your tears, Terentianus. Here is balm for your anguish. Look! Your son has recovered his health and his reason through the intercession of the martyrs.

TERENTIANUS. Praise to the Eternal King Who covers His servants with such glory! Not only do their souls rejoice in heaven, but in the depths of the sepulchre their lifeless bones work astounding miracles, testifying to their sanctity and to the grace of our Lord Jesus Christ Who liveth and reigneth!

DULCITIUS

ARGUMENT

THE martyrdom of the holy virgins Agape, Chionia, and
Irena. The Governor Dulcitius seeks them out in the
silence of the night with criminal intent, but hardly has
he entered their dwelling than he becomes the victim of a
delusion, under which he mistakes for the objects of his
passion the saucepans and frying-pans in the kitchen.
These he embraces and covers with kisses until his face
and clothes are black with soot and dirt. Later, by order
of Diocletian, he hands the maidens over to the care of
Sisinnius, who is charged with their punishment. Sisinnius in his turn is made the sport of the most strange
delusions, but at length succeeds in getting Agape and
Chionia burnt, and Irena shot to death with arrows.

CHARACTERS

THE EMPEROR DIOCLETIAN.
AGAPE.
CHIONIA.
IRENA.
DULCITIUS (*Governor of Thessalonica*).
SOLDIERS.
SISINNIUS.
WIFE TO DULCITIUS.
> *Ushers of the Imperial Palace.*
> *Ladies-in-Waiting on the Wife of Dulcitius.*

DULCITIUS

SCENE I

DIOCLETIAN. The pure and famous race to which you belong and your own rare beauty make it fitting that you should be wedded to the highest in our court. Thus we decree, making the condition that you first promise to deny your Christ and sacrifice to the gods.

AGAPE. We beg you not to concern yourself about us, and it is useless to make preparations for our marriage. Nothing can make us deny that Name which all should confess, or let our purity be stained.

DIOCLETIAN. What does this madness mean?

AGAPE. What sign of madness do you see in us?

DIOCLETIAN. It is clear enough.

AGAPE. In what way are we mad?

DIOCLETIAN. Is it not madness to give up practising an ancient religion and run after this silly new Christian superstition?

AGAPE. You are bold to slander the majesty of Almighty God. It is dangerous.

DIOCLETIAN. Dangerous? To whom?

AGAPE. To you, and to the state you rule.

DIOCLETIAN. The girl raves. Take her away.

CHIONIA. My sister does not rave. She is right.

DIOCLETIAN. This mænad seems even more violent than the other! Remove her also from our presence, and we will question the third.

IRENA. You will find her as rebellious and as determined to resist.

DIOCLETIAN. Irena, you are the youngest in years. Show yourself the oldest in dignity.

IRENA. Pray tell me how.

DIOCLETIAN. Bow your head to the gods, and set an example to your sisters. It may rebuke and save them.

IRENA. Let those who wish to provoke the wrath of the Most High prostrate themselves before idols! I will not dishonour this head which has been anointed with heavenly oil by abasing it at the feet of images.

DIOCLETIAN. The worship of the gods does not bring dishonour to those who practise it, but, on the contrary, the greatest honour.

IRENA. What could be more shameful baseness, what baser shame, than to venerate slaves as if they were lords?

DIOCLETIAN. I do not ask you to worship slaves, but the gods of princes and the rulers of the earth.

IRENA. A god who can be bought cheap in the market-place, what is he but a slave?

DIOCLETIAN. Enough of this presumptuous chatter. The rack shall put an end to it!

IRENA. That is what we desire. We ask nothing better than to suffer the most cruel tortures for the love of Christ.

DIOCLETIAN. Let these obstinate women who dare to defy our authority be laden with chains and thrown into a dungeon. Let them be examined by Governor Dulcitius.

SCENE II

DULCITIUS. Soldiers, produce your prisoners.

SOLDIERS. The ones you wanted to see are in there.

DULCITIUS. Ye Gods, but these girls are beautiful! What grace, what charm!

SOLDIERS. Perfect!

DULCITIUS. I am enraptured!

SOLDIERS. No wonder!

DULCITIUS. I'm in love! Do you think they will fall in love with me?

SOLDIERS. From what we know, you will have little success.

DULCITIUS. Why?

SOLDIERS. Their faith is too strong.

DULCITIUS. A few sweet words will work wonders!

SOLDIERS. They despise flattery.

DULCITIUS. Then I shall woo in another fashion—with torture !

SOLDIERS. They would not care.

DULCITIUS. What's to be done, then ?

SOLDIERS. That is for you to find out.

DULCITIUS. Lock them in the inner room—the one leading out of the passage where the pots and pans are kept.

SOLDIERS. Why there ?

DULCITIUS. I can visit them oftener.

SOLDIERS. It shall be done.

SCENE III

DULCITIUS. What can the prisoners be doing at this hour of night ?

SOLDIERS. They pass the time singing hymns.

DULCITIUS. Let us approach.

SOLDIERS. Now you can hear their silver-sweet voices in the distance.

DULCITIUS. Take your torches, and guard the doors. I will go in and enjoy myself in those lovely arms !

SOLDIERS. Enter. We will wait for you here.

SCENE IV

AGAPE. What noise is that outside the door ?

IRENA. It is that wretch Dulcitius.

CHIONIA. Now may God protect us!

AGAPE. Amen.

CHIONIA. There is more noise! It sounds like the clashing of pots and pans and fire-irons.

IRENA. I will go and look. Come quick and peep through the crack of the door!

AGAPE. What is it?

IRENA. Oh, look! He must be out of his senses! I believe he thinks that he is kissing us.

AGAPE. What is he doing?

IRENA. Now he presses the saucepans tenderly to his breast, now the kettles and frying-pans! He is kissing them hard!

CHIONIA. How absurd!

IRENA. His face, his hands, his clothes! They are all as black as soot. He looks like an Ethiope.

AGAPE. I am glad. His body should turn black— to match his soul, which is possessed of a devil.

IRENA. Look! He is going now. Let us watch the soldiers and see what they do when he goes out.

SCENE V

SOLDIERS. What's this? Either one possessed by the devil, or the devil himself. Let's be off!

DULCITIUS. Soldiers, soldiers! Why do you hurry away? Stay, wait! Light me to my house with your torches.

SOLDIERS. The voice is our master's voice, but the face is a devil's. Come, let's take to our heels ! This devil means us no good.

DULCITIUS. I will hasten to the palace. I will tell the whole court how I have been insulted.

SCENE VI

DULCITIUS. Ushers, admit me at once. I have important business with the Emperor.

USHERS. Who is this fearsome, horrid monster ? Coming here in these filthy rags ! Come, let us beat him and throw him down the steps. Stop him from coming further.

DULCITIUS. Ye gods, what has happened to me ? Am I not dressed in my best ? Am I not clean and fine in my person ? And yet everyone who meets me expresses disgust at the sight of me and treats me as if I were some foul monster ! I will go to my wife. She will tell me the truth. But here she comes. Her looks are wild, her hair unbound, and all her household follow her weeping.

SCENE VII

WIFE OF DULCITIUS. My lord, my lord, what evil has come on you ? Have you lost your reason, Dulcitius ? Have the Christ-worshippers put a spell on you ?

DULCITIUS. Now at last I know ! Those artful women have made an ass of me !

WIFE OF DULCITIUS. What troubled me most, and made my heart ache, was that you should not know there was anything amiss with you.

DULCITIUS. Those impudent wenches shall be stripped and exposed naked in public. They shall have a taste of the outrage to which I have been subjected !

SCENE VIII

SOLDIERS. Here we are sweating like pigs and what's the use ? Their clothes cling to their bodies like their own skin. What's more, our chief, who ordered us to strip them, sits there snoring, and there's no way of waking him. We will go to the Emperor and tell him all that has passed.

SCENE IX

DIOCLETIAN. I grieve to hear of the outrageous way in which the Governor Dulcitius has been insulted and hoaxed ! But these girls shall not boast of having blasphemed our gods with impunity, or of having made a mock of those who worship them. I will entrust the execution of my vengeance to Count Sisinnius.

SCENE X

SISINNIUS. Soldiers, where are these impudent hussies who are to be put to the torture ?

SOLDIERS. In there.

SISINNIUS. Keep Irena back, and bring the others here.

SOLDIERS. Why is one to be treated differently ?

SISINNIUS. She is young, and besides she may be more easily influenced when not intimidated by her sisters.

SOLDIERS. That may be so.

SCENE XI

SOLDIERS. We have brought the girls you asked for.

SISINNIUS. Agape, and you, Chionia, take my advice.

AGAPE. And if we do, what then ?

SISINNIUS. You will sacrifice to the gods.

AGAPE. We offer a perpetual sacrifice of praise to the true God, the eternal Father, to His Son, co-eternal, and to the Holy Ghost.

SISINNIUS. I do not speak of that sacrifice. That is prohibited on pain of the most severe penalties.

AGAPE. You have no power over us, and can never compel us to sacrifice to demons.

SISINNIUS. Do not be obstinate. Sacrifice to the gods, or by order of the Emperor Diocletian I must put you to death.

CHIONIA. Your Emperor has ordered you to put us to death, and you must obey, as we scorn his decree. If you were to spare us out of pity, you also would die.

SISINNIUS. Come, soldiers! Seize these blasphemers and fling them alive into the flames.

SOLDIERS. We will build a pyre at once. The fierceness of the fire will soon put an end to their insolence.

AGAPE. O Lord, we know Thy power! It would not be anything strange or new if the fire forgot its nature and obeyed Thee. But we are weary of this world, and we implore Thee to break the bonds that chain our souls, and to let our bodies be consumed that we may rejoice with Thee in heaven.

SOLDIERS. O wonderful, most wonderful! Their spirits have left their bodies, but there is no sign of any hurt. Neither their hair, nor their garments, much less their bodies, have been touched by the flames!

SISINNIUS. Bring Irena here.

SOLDIERS. There she is.

SCENE XII

SISINNIUS. Irena, take warning from the fate of your sisters, and tremble, for if you follow their example you will perish.

IRENA. I long to follow their example, and to die, that I may share their eternal joy.

SISINNIUS. Yield, yield !

IRENA. I will yield to no man who persuades me to sin.

SISINNIUS. If you persist in your refusal, I shall not grant you a swift death. I shall eke it out, and every day I shall increase and renew your torments.

IRENA. The greater my pain, the greater my glory !

SISINNIUS. You are not afraid of being tortured, I know, but I can use another means that will be abhorrent to you.

IRENA. By Christ's help I shall escape from all you can devise against me.

SISINNIUS. I can send you to a house of ill-fame, where your body will be abominably defiled.

IRENA. Better far that my body should suffer outrage than my soul.

SISINNIUS. When you are dishonoured and forced to live among harlots, you can no longer be numbered among the virgins.

IRENA. The wage of sin is death ; the wage of suffering a crown. If the soul does not consent, there is no guilt.

SISINNIUS. In vain I try to spare her, and show pity to her youth !

SOLDIERS. We could have told you as much. She is not to be frightened, and nothing can make her worship the gods.

SISINNIUS. I will show her no more mercy.

SOLDIERS. That is the only way to deal with her.

SISINNIUS. Have no pity. Be rough with her, and drag her to the lowest brothel you can find.

IRENA. They will never take me there.

SISINNIUS. Indeed ! What can prevent them ?

IRENA. The power that rules the world.

SISINNIUS. We shall see.

IRENA. Yes ! Sooner than you will like !

SISINNIUS. Soldiers, do not let the absurd prophecies of this woman interfere with your duty.

SOLDIERS. We are not likely to be frightened by a slip of a girl ! We will carry out your orders at once.

SCENE XIII

SISINNIUS. Who are these men hurrying towards us ? They cannot be the soldiers who took away Irena. Yet they resemble them. Yes, these are the men ! Why have you returned so suddenly ? Why are you panting for breath ?

SOLDIERS. We ran back to find you.

SISINNIUS. Where is the girl ?

SOLDIERS. On the crest of the mountain.

SISINNIUS. What mountain ?

SOLDIERS. The mountain yonder, nearest this place.

SISINNIUS. O fools, madmen ! Have you lost your senses ?

SOLDIERS. What's the matter? Why do you look at us so threateningly, and speak with such anger?

SISINNIUS. May the gods crush you with their thunder!

SOLDIERS. What have we done? How have we offended? We have only obeyed your orders.

SISINNIUS. Fools! Did I not tell you to take this rebellious girl to a brothel?

SOLDIERS. That is so, but while we were on the way up came two young strangers and told us you had sent them to take Irena to the summit of the mountain.

SISINNIUS. I learn this for the first time from you.

SOLDIERS. So we see.

SISINNIUS. What were these strangers like?

SOLDIERS. They were gorgeously dressed and looked like people of rank.

SISINNIUS. Did you not follow them?

SOLDIERS. Yes, we followed them.

SISINNIUS. What did they do?

SOLDIERS. They placed themselves one on each side of Irena, and told us to hasten and tell you what we had seen.

SISINNIUS. Then there is nothing to do but for me to mount my horse and ride to the mountain to discover who has dared to play us this trick.

SOLDIERS. We will come too.

SCENE XIV

SISINNIUS. What has happened to me? These Christians have bewitched me. I wander blindly round this hill, and when I stumble on a path I can neither follow it nor return upon my steps.

SOLDIERS. We are all the sport of some strange enchantment. We are exhausted. If you let this mad-woman live an hour longer it will be the death of us all.

SISINNIUS. Take a bow one of you, bend it as far as you can, and loose a shaft that shall pierce this devilish witch.

SOLDIERS. That's the way!

IRENA. You wretched Sisinnius! Do you not blush for your shameful defeat? Are you not ashamed that you could not overcome the resolution of a little child without resorting to force of arms?

SISINNIUS. I accept the shame gladly, since now I am sure of your death.

IRENA. To me my death means joy, but to you calamity. For your cruelty you will be damned in Tartarus. But I shall receive the martyr's palm, and, adorned with the crown of virginity, I shall enter the azure palace of the Eternal King, to Whom be glory and honour for ever and ever!

CALLIMACHUS

ARGUMENT

THE resurrection of Drusiana and Callimachus.

Callimachus cherishes a guilty passion for Drusiana, not only while she is alive but after she has died in the Lord. He dies from the bite of a serpent, but, thanks to the prayers of Saint John the Apostle, he is restored to life, together with Drusiana, and is born again in Christ.

CHARACTERS

CALLIMACHUS.
FRIENDS TO CALLIMACHUS.
DRUSIANA.
ANDRONICUS.
FORTUNATUS.
THE APOSTLE JOHN.

CALLIMACHUS

SCENE I

CALLIMACHUS. My friends, a word with you.

FRIENDS. We are at your service as long as you please.

CALLIMACHUS. I should prefer to speak with you apart from the crowd.

FRIENDS. What pleases you, pleases us.

CALLIMACHUS. Then we will go to some quieter place where no one will interrupt us.

FRIENDS. Just as you like.

SCENE II

CALLIMACHUS. For a long time now I have been in great trouble. I hope that by confiding in you I shall find relief.

FRIENDS. When a man tells his friends of his sufferings it is only fair that they should try to share them.

CALLIMACHUS. I would to heaven that you could lighten this load upon my heart !

FRIENDS. Well, tell us precisely what is wrong. We will grieve with you, if we must. If not, we can do our best to distract your mind.

CALLIMACHUS. I love——

FRIENDS. What do you love?

CALLIMACHUS. A thing of beauty, a thing of grace!

FRIENDS. That is too vague! How can we tell from this what is the object of your love?

CALLIMACHUS. Woman.

FRIENDS. Ah, now you say "woman" we all understand!

CALLIMACHUS. By woman, I mean a woman.

FRIENDS. Clearer still! But it is impossible to give an opinion on a subject until the subject is defined. So name the woman.

CALLIMACHUS. Drusiana.

FRIENDS. What? The wife of Prince Andronicus?

CALLIMACHUS. Yes.

FRIENDS. Nothing can come of that. She has been baptized.

CALLIMACHUS. What do I care, if I can win her love?

FRIENDS. You cannot.

CALLIMACHUS. What makes you say so?

FRIENDS. You are crying for the moon.

CALLIMACHUS. Am I the first to do so? Have I not the example of many others to encourage me?

FRIENDS. Now listen. This woman you sigh for is a follower of the holy Apostle John, and has devoted herself entirely to God. They say she will not even go to the bed of Andronicus although he is a devout Christian. Is it likely that she will listen to you ?

CALLIMACHUS. I came to you for consolation, and instead you drive me to despair !

FRIENDS. We should be poor friends if we consoled and flattered you at the expense of the truth.

CALLIMACHUS. Since you refuse to advise me, I will go to her and pour out my soul in words that would melt a heart of stone !

FRIENDS. Fool ! it is hopeless !

CALLIMACHUS. I defy the stars !

FRIENDS. We shall see.

SCENE III

CALLIMACHUS. Drusiana, listen to me ! Drusiana, my deepest heart's love !

DRUSIANA. Your words amaze me, Callimachus. What can you want of me ?

CALLIMACHUS. You are amazed ?

DRUSIANA. I am astounded.

CALLIMACHUS. First I want to speak of love !

DRUSIANA. Love ! What love ?

CALLIMACHUS. That love with which I love you above all created things.

DRUSIANA. Why should you love me ? You are not of my kin. There is no legal bond between us.

CALLIMACHUS. It is your beauty.

DRUSIANA. My beauty ?

CALLIMACHUS. Yes.

DRUSIANA. What is my beauty to you ?

CALLIMACHUS. But little now—it is that which tortures me—but I hope that it may be much before long.

DRUSIANA. Not a word more.   Leave me at once, for it is a sin to listen to you now that I understand your devilish meaning.

CALLIMACHUS. My Drusiana, do not kill me with your looks.   Do not drive away one who worships you, but give back love for love.

DRUSIANA. Wicked, insidious words !   They fall on deaf ears.   Your love disgusts me.   Understand I despise you !

CALLIMACHUS. You cannot make me angry, because I know that you would own my passion moves you if you were not ashamed.

DRUSIANA. It moves me to indignation, nothing else.

CALLIMACHUS. That feeling will not last.

DRUSIANA. I shall not change, be sure of that.

CALLIMACHUS. I would not be too sure.

DRUSIANA. You frantic, foolish man ! Do not deceive yourself !   Why delude yourself with vain hopes ? What madness leads you to think that I shall yield ? I have renounced even what is lawful—my husband's bed !

CALLIMACHUS. I call heaven and earth to witness that if you do not yield I will never rest from the fight for you. I will be as cunning as the serpent. I will use all my skill and strength to trap you.

SCENE IV

DRUSIANA. O Lord Jesus, what use is my vow of chastity? My beauty has all the same made this man love me. Pity my fears, O Lord. Pity the grief which has seized me. I know not what to do. If I tell anyone what has happened, there will be disorder in the city on my account; if I keep silence, only Thy grace can protect me from falling into the net spread for me. O Christ, take me to Thyself. Let me die swiftly. Save me from being the ruin of a soul!

ANDRONICUS. Drusiana, Drusiana! Christ, what blow has fallen on me! Drusiana is dead. Run one of you and fetch the holy man John.

SCENE V

JOHN. Why do you weep, my son?

ANDRONICUS. Oh, horrible! O Lord, that life should suddenly become so hateful!

JOHN. What troubles you?

ANDRONICUS. Drusiana, your disciple, Drusiana—

JOHN. She has passed from the sight of men?

ANDRONICUS. Yes. And I am desolate.

JOHN. It is not right to mourn so bitterly for those whose souls we know rejoice in peace.

ANDRONICUS. God knows I do not doubt that her soul is in eternal joy, and that her incorrupt body will rise again. What grieves me so sorely is that in my presence just now she prayed for death. She begged she might die.

JOHN. You know her reason ?

ANDRONICUS. I know it, and will tell you when I am less sick with grief.

JOHN. Come. We must celebrate the funeral rites with proper ceremony.

ANDRONICUS. There is a marble tomb near here in which the body shall be laid, and our steward Fortunatus shall guard her grave.

JOHN. It is right that she should be interred with honour. God rest her soul in peace.

SCENE VI

CALLIMACHUS. Fortunatus, Fortunatus, what is to become of me ? Death itself cannot quench my love for Drusiana !

FORTUNATUS. Poor wretch !

CALLIMACHUS. I shall die if you do not help me.

FORTUNATUS. How can I help you ?

CALLIMACHUS. In this. You can let me look on her, dead.

FORTUNATUS. Up to now the body is sound and whole, I reckon because it was not wasted with disease. As you know she was taken in a moment by a fever.

CALLIMACHUS. Oh, how happy I should be if I might see for myself.

FORTUNATUS. If you are willing to pay me well, you can do what you like.

CALLIMACHUS. Here, take all I have with me, and be sure that I will give you more, much more, later.

FORTUNATUS. Quick, then! We'll go to the tomb.

CALLIMACHUS. You cannot go quickly enough for me.

SCENE VII

FORTUNATUS. There lies the body. The face is not like the face of a corpse. The limbs show no sign of decay. You can take her to your heart.

CALLIMACHUS. O Drusiana, Drusiana, I worshipped you with my whole soul! I yearned from my very bowels to embrace you! And you repulsed me, and thwarted my desire. Now you are in my power, now I can wound you with my kisses, and pour out my love on you.

FORTUNATUS. Take care! A monstrous serpent! It is coming towards us!

CALLIMACHUS. A curse on me! And on you, Fortunatus, who led me on and urged me to this infamy. Wretch, may you die from the serpent's bite! Terror and remorse are killing me.

SCENE VIII

JOHN. Come, Andronicus, let us go to Drusiana's tomb, and commend her soul to Christ in prayer.

ANDRONICUS. It is like your holiness not to forget one who trusted in you.

JOHN. Behold ! The invisible God appears to us, made visible in the form of a beautiful youth.

ANDRONICUS (*To the Spectators*). Tremble.*

JOHN. Lord Jesus, why hast Thou deigned to manifest Thyself to Thy servants in this place ?

GOD. To raise Drusiana from the dead, and with her him who lies outside her tomb, have I come, that in them My Name may be glorified.

ANDRONICUS. How swiftly He was caught up again into heaven !

JOHN. I cannot altogether understand what this means.

ANDRONICUS. Let us go on to the tomb. It may be that there what is now obscure will become clear.

SCENE IX

JOHN. In Christ's name, what miracle is this ? The sepulchre is open, and Drusiana's body has been cast

---

* This admonition to " spectators " is in the MS. and seems inexplicable if Roswitha wrote her plays to be read, not performed.

forth. And near it lie two other corpses enlaced in a serpent's coils.

ANDRONICUS. I begin to understand. This is Callimachus, who while he lived was consumed with an unholy passion for Drusiana. It troubled her greatly and her distress brought on a fever. She prayed that she might die.

JOHN. Such was her love of chastity.

ANDRONICUS. After her death the wretched man, crazed with love, and stung by the defeat of his wicked plan, was still more inflamed by desire.

JOHN. Pitiable creature!

ANDRONICUS. I have no doubt that he bribed this unworthy servant to give him the opportunity for committing a detestable crime.

JOHN. It is not to be believed!

ANDRONICUS. But death struck both of them down before the deed was accomplished.

JOHN. They met their deserts.

ANDRONICUS. What astonishes me most is that the Divine Voice should have promised the resurrection of him who planned the crime, and not of him who was only an accomplice. Maybe it is because the one, blinded by the passion of the flesh, knew not what he did, while the other sinned of deliberate malice.

JOHN. With what wonderful exactness the Supreme Judge examines the deeds of men! How even the scales in which He weighs the merits of each individual man ! None can understand, none explain. Human wisdom cannot grasp the subtlety of the divine judgment.

ANDRONICUS. So we should be content to marvel at it, as it is not in our power to attain a precise knowledge of the causes of things.

JOHN. Often the sequel teaches us to understand better.

ANDRONICUS. Then, blessed John, do now what you were told to do. Raise Callimachus to life, and the knot of our perplexity may be untied.

JOHN. First I must invoke the name of Christ to drive away the serpent. Then Callimachus shall be raised.

ANDRONICUS. You are right; else the venom of the creature might do him fresh injury.

JOHN. Hence, savage monster ! Away from this man, for now he is to serve Christ.

ANDRONICUS. Although the beast has no reason, it heeds your command.

JOHN. Not through my power, but through Christ's, it obeys me.

ANDRONICUS. Look ! As swift as thought it has vanished !

JOHN. O God, the world cannot contain nor the mind of man comprehend the wonders of Thy incalculable unity, Thou Who alone art what Thou art ! O Thou Who by mingling different elements canst create man, and by separating those elements again canst dissolve him, grant that the spirit and the body of this Callimachus may be joined once more, and that he may rise again wholly as he was, so that all looking on him may praise Thee, Who alone canst work miracles !

ANDRONICUS. Look ! The breath of life stirs in him again, but he does not move.

JOHN. Callimachus ! In the name of Christ, arise, and confess your sin ! Do not keep back the smallest grain of the truth.

CALLIMACHUS. I cannot deny that I came here for an evil purpose, but the pangs of love consumed me. I was beside myself.

JOHN. What mad folly possessed you ? That you should dare think of such a shameful outrage to the chaste dead !

CALLIMACHUS. Yes, I was mad ; but this knave Fortunatus led me on.

JOHN. And now, most miserable man, confess ! Were you so vile as to do what you desired ?

CALLIMACHUS. No ! I could think of it, but I could not do it.

JOHN. What prevented you ?

CALLIMACHUS. I had hardly touched the lifeless body—I had hardly drawn aside the shroud, when that fellow there, who has been the spark to my fire, died from the serpent's poison.

ANDRONICUS. A good riddance !

CALLIMACHUS. At the same moment there

appeared to me a young man, beautiful yet terrible, who reverently covered the corpse again. From his flaming face and breast burning coals flew out, and one of them, falling on me, touched my face. I heard a voice say, " Callimachus, die to live ! " It was then I breathed my last.

JOHN. Oh, heavenly grace ! God delights not in the damnation of the wicked.

CALLIMACHUS. You have heard the dreadful tale of my temptation. I beg you not to delay the merciful remedy.

JOHN. I will not delay it.

CALLIMACHUS. I am overwhelmed by the thought of my abominable crime. I repent with my whole heart, and bewail my sin.

JOHN. That is but right, for a great fault must be atoned for by a great repentance.

CALLIMACHUS. Oh, if I could lay bare my heart and show you the bitter anguish I suffer, you would pity me !

JOHN. Not so. Rather does your suffering fill me with joy, for I know that it will be your salvation.

CALLIMACHUS. I loathe the delights of the flesh, and all the sins of my past life.

JOHN. That is well.

CALLIMACHUS. I truly repent my foul deed.

JOHN. Again that is well.

CALLIMACHUS. I am filled with such remorse

that I have no desire to live unless I can be born again in Christ and changed.

JOHN. I do not doubt that heavenly grace is at work in you.

CALLIMACHUS. Oh, hasten then to help a man in dire need ! Give me some comfort ! Help me to throw off the grief which crushes me ! Show me how a Pagan may change into a Christian, a fornicator into a chaste man ! Oh, set my feet on the way of truth ! Teach me to live mindful of the divine promises !

JOHN. Now blessed be the only Son of God, Who made Himself partaker of our frailty, and showed you mercy, my son Callimachus, by striking you down with the death which has brought you to the true life. So has He saved the creature He made in His own image from the death of the soul.

ANDRONICUS. Most strange, most wonderful miracle !

JOHN. O Christ, redemption of the world, and sinners' atonement, I have no words to praise Thee ! The sweetness of Thy compassion amazes me. Now Thou dost win the sinner with gentleness, now Thou dost chastise him with just severity, and callest on him to do penance.

ANDRONICUS. Glory to His divine goodness !

JOHN. Who would have presumed to hope that a man like this, intent on a wicked deed when death over-took him, would be raised to life again, and given the chance of making reparation ! Blessed be Thy name for ever and ever, O Thou Who alone canst do these wondrous things !

ANDRONICUS.   Holy John, give me some comfort too. The love I bear my dead wife will not let me rest until I have seen her also called back from the dead.

JOHN. Drusiana, our Lord Jesus Christ calls you back to life !

DRUSIANA. Glory and praise to Thee, O Lord, Who hast made me live again !

CALLIMACHUS. Thanks be to that merciful power, my Drusiana, through which you, who left this life in such sorrow, rise again in joy !

DRUSIANA. Venerable father John, you have restored to life Callimachus, who loved me sinfully. Should you not also raise from the dead the man who betrayed my buried body ?

CALLIMACHUS. Apostle of Christ, do not believe it ! Will you release from the fetters of death this evil creature, this traitor, who led me away and persuaded me to venture on that horrible deed ?

JOHN. You should not wish to deprive him of divine mercy, my son.

CALLIMACHUS. He tried to ruin me ! He is not worthy of resurrection !

JOHN. We are taught by our faith that man must forgive his fellow-man if he would be forgiven by God.

ANDRONICUS. That is true.

JOHN. Remember that when the only Son of God, the Virgin's first-born, the one man born without a stain, came into this world, He found us all bowed under the heavy weight of sin.

ANDRONICUS. True again.

JOHN. And though not one of us was guiltless, He deprived no one of His mercy, but offered Himself for all, and for all laid down His life in love.

ANDRONICUS. Had the Innocent One not been slain, none of us would have been saved.

JOHN. He cannot rejoice in the damnation of those whom He bought with His blood.

ANDRONICUS. To Him be praise !

JOHN. This is why we must not grudge the grace of God to anyone. It is no merit of ours if it abounds in ourselves.

CALLIMACHUS. Your rebuke makes me ashamed.

JOHN. Yet it is not for me to oppose you. Drusiana, inspired by God Himself shall raise this man.

DRUSIANA. Divine Essence without material form, Who hast made man in Thine own image and breathed into this clay the spirit of life, bring back the vital heat to the body of Fortunatus, that our triple resurrection may glorify the adorable Trinity.

JOHN. Amen.

DRUSIANA. Fortunatus, awake, and in the name of Christ burst the bonds of death.

FORTUNATUS. Who wakes me ? Who takes my hand ? Who calls me back to life ?

JOHN. Drusiana.

FORTUNATUS. How can that be ? Only a few days since she died.

JOHN. Yes, but now, through the power of Christ, she lives again.

FORTUNATUS. And is that Callimachus who stands there ? By his sober and pious look one would think he is no longer dying of love for his Drusiana !

JOHN. All that is changed. Now he loves and serves Christ.

FORTUNATUS. No !

JOHN. It is true.

FORTUNATUS. If it is as you say, if Drusiana has restored me to life and Callimachus believes in Christ, I reject life and choose death. I would rather not exist than see them swelling with grace and virtue !

JOHN. Oh, incredible envy of the devil ! Oh, malice of the old serpent, who since he made our first parents taste death has never ceased to writhe at the glory of the righteous ! Oh, Fortunatus, brimful of Satan's bitter gall, how much do you resemble the rotten tree that, bearing only bad fruit, must be cut down and cast into the fire ! To the fire you must go, where, deprived of the society of those who fear God, you will be tormented without respite for ever.

ANDRONICUS. Look ! Oh, look ! His wounds

have opened again.   He has been taken at his word.   He is dying.

JOHN.   Let him die and go down to hell, who through envious spite rejected the gift of life.

ANDRONICUS.   A terrible fate.

JOHN.   Nothing is more terrible than envy, nothing more evil than pride.

ANDRONICUS.   Both are vile.

JOHN.   The man who is the victim of one is the victim of the other, for they have no separate existence.

ANDRONICUS.   Please explain.

JOHN.   The proud are envious, and the envious are proud.   A jealous man cannot endure to hear others praised, and seeks to belittle those who are more perfect. He disdains to take a lower place, and arrogantly seeks to be put above his equals.

ANDRONICUS.   That is clear.

JOHN.   This wretched man's pride was wounded. He could not endure the humiliation of recognizing his inferiority to these two in whom he could not deny God had made more grace to shine.

ANDRONICUS.   I understand now why his resurrection was not spoken of.   It was known he would die again

JOHN.   He deserved to die twice, for to his crime of profaning the sacred grave entrusted to him, he added hatred and envy of those who had been restored to life.

ANDRONICUS.   The wretched creature is dead now.

JOHN. Come, let us go—Satan must have his own. This day shall be kept as a festival in thanksgiving for the wonderful conversion of Callimachus. Men shall long speak of it, and of his resurrection from the dead, and of Drusiana, on whom his love brought misery. Let us give thanks to God, that just and penetrating Judge Who alone can search the heart and reins and reward or punish fairly. To Him alone be honour, strength, glory, praise, and blessing, world without end. Amen.

ABRAHAM

ARGUMENT

THE fall and repentance of Mary, the niece of the hermit Abraham, who, after she has spent twenty years in the religious life as a solitary, abandons it in despair, and, returning to the world, does not shrink from becoming a harlot.   But two years later Abraham, in the disguise of a lover, seeks her out and reclaims her.   For twenty years she does penance for her sins with many tears, fastings, vigils, and prayers.

CHARACTERS

ABRAHAM.
EPHREM.
MARY.
A FRIEND TO ABRAHAM.
AN INN-KEEPER.

ABRAHAM

SCENE I

ABRAHAM. Brother Ephrem, my dear comrade in the hermit life, may I speak to you now, or shall I wait until you have finished your divine praises ?

EPHREM. And what can you have to say to me which is not praise of Him Who said : " Where two or three are gathered together in My Name, I am with them " ?

ABRAHAM. I have not come to speak of anything which He would not like to hear.

EPHREM. I am sure of it. So speak at once.

ABRAHAM. It concerns a decision I have to make. I long for your approval.

EPHREM. We have one heart and one soul. We ought to agree.

ABRAHAM. I have a little niece of tender years. She has lost both her parents, and my affection for her has been deepened by compassion for her lonely state. I am in constant anxiety on her account.

EPHREM. Ought you who have triumphed over the world to be vexed by its cares !

ABRAHAM. My only care is her radiant beauty! What if it should one day be dimmed by sin.

EPHREM. No one can blame you for being anxious.

ABRAHAM. I hope not.

EPHREM. How old is she?

ABRAHAM. At the end of this year she will be eight.

EPHREM. She is very young.

ABRAHAM. That does not lessen my anxiety.

EPHREM. Where does she live?

ABRAHAM. At my hermitage now; for at the request of her other kinsfolk I have undertaken to bring her up. The fortune left her ought, I think, to be given to the poor.

EPHREM. A mind taught so early to despise temporal things should be fixed on heaven.

ABRAHAM. I desire with all my heart to see her the spouse of Christ and devoted entirely to His service.

EPHREM. A praiseworthy wish.

ABRAHAM. I was inspired by her name.

EPHREM. What is she called?

ABRAHAM. Mary.

EPHREM. Mary! Such a name ought to be adorned with the crown of virginity.

ABRAHAM. I have no fear that she will be unwilling, but we must be gentle.

EPHREM. Come, let us go, and impress on her that no life is so sweet and secure as the religious one.

SCENE II

ABRAHAM. Mary, my child by adoption, whom I love as my own soul !   Listen to my advice as to a father's, and to Brother Ephrem's as that of a very wise man. Strive to imitate the chastity of the holy Virgin whose name you bear.

EPHREM. Child, would it not be a shame if you, who through the mystery of your name are called to mount to the stars where Mary the mother of God reigns, chose instead the low pleasures of the earth ?

MARY. I know nothing about the mystery of my name, so how can I tell what you mean ?

EPHREM. Mary, my child, means " star of the sea " —that star which rules the world and all the peoples in the world.

MARY. Why is it called the star of the sea ?

EPHREM. Because it never sets, but shines always in the heavens to show mariners their right course.

MARY. And how can such a poor thing as I am— made out of slime, as my uncle says—shine like my name ?

EPHREM. By keeping your body unspotted, and your mind pure and holy.

MARY. It would be too great an honour for any human being to become like the stars.

EPHREM. If you choose you can be as the angels of

God, and when at last you cast off the burden of this mortal body they will be near you. With them you will pass through the air, and walk on the sky. With them you will sweep round the zodiac, and never slacken your steps until the Virgin's Son takes you in His arms in His mother's dazzling bridal room !

MARY. Who but an ass would think little of such happiness ! So I choose to despise the things of earth, and deny myself now that I may enjoy it !

EPHREM. Out of the mouths of babes and sucklings ! A childish heart, but a mature mind !

ABRAHAM. God be thanked for it !

EPHREM. Amen to that.

ABRAHAM. But though by God's grace she has been given the light, at her tender age she must be taught how to use it.

EPHREM. You are right.

ABRAHAM. I will build her a little cell with a narrow entrance near my hermitage. I can visit her there often, and through the window instruct her in the psalter and other pages of the divine law.

EPHREM. That is a good plan.

MARY. I put myself under your direction, Father Ephrem.

EPHREM. My daughter ! May the Heavenly Bridegroom to Whom you have given yourself in the tender bud of your youth shield you from the wiles of the devil !

SCENE III

ABRAHAM. Brother Ephrem, Brother Ephrem! When anything happens, good or bad, it is to you I turn. It is your counsel I seek. Do not turn your face away, brother—do not be impatient, but help me.

EPHREM. Abraham, Abraham, what has come to you? What is the cause of this immoderate grief? Ought a hermit to weep and groan after the manner of the world?

ABRAHAM. Was any hermit ever so stricken? I cannot bear my sorrow.

EPHREM. Brother, no more of this. To the point; what has happened?

ABRAHAM. Mary! Mary! my adopted child! Mary, whom I cared for so lovingly and taught with all my skill for ten years! Mary——

EPHREM. Well, what is it?

ABRAHAM. Oh God! She is lost!

EPHREM. Lost? What do you mean?

ABRAHAM. Most miserably. Afterwards she ran away.

EPHREM. But by what wiles did the ancient enemy bring about her undoing?

ABRAHAM. By the wiles of false love. Dressed in a monk's habit, the hypocrite went to see her often. He succeeded in making the poor ignorant child love him. She leapt from the window of her cell for an evil deed.

EPHREM. I shudder as I listen to you.

ABRAHAM. When the unhappy girl knew that she was ruined, she beat her breast and dug her nails into her face. She tore her garments, pulled out her hair. Her despairing cries were terrible to hear.

EPHREM. I am not surprised. For such a fall a whole fountain of tears should rise.

ABRAHAM. She moaned out that she could never be the same——

EPHREM. Poor, miserable girl!

ABRAHAM. And reproached herself for having forgotten our warning.

EPHREM. She might well do so.

ABRAHAM. She cried that all her vigils, prayers, and fasts had been thrown away.

EPHREM. If she perseveres in this penitence she will be saved.

ABRAHAM. She has not persevered. She has added worse to her evil deed.

EPHREM. Oh, this moves me to the depths of my heart!

ABRAHAM. After all these tears and lamentations she was overcome by remorse, and fell headlong into the abyss of despair.

EPHREM. A bitter business!

ABRAHAM. She despaired of being able to win pardon, and resolved to go back to the world and its vanities.

EPHREM. I cannot remember when the devil could boast of such a triumph over the hermits.

ABRAHAM. Now we are at the mercy of the demons.

EPHREM. I marvel that she could have escaped without your knowledge.

ABRAHAM. If I had not been so blind! I ought to have paid more heed to that terrible vision. Yes, I see now that it was sent to warn me.

EPHREM. What vision?

ABRAHAM. I dreamed I was standing at the door of my cell, and that a huge dragon with a loathsome stench rushed violently towards me. I saw that the creature was attracted by a little white dove at my side. It pounced on the dove, devoured it, and vanished.

EPHREM. There is no doubt what this vision meant.

ABRAHAM. When I woke I turned over in my mind what I had seen, and took it as a sign of some persecution threatening the Church, through which many of the faithful would be drawn into error. I prostrated myself in prayer, and implored Him Who knows the future to enlighten me.

EPHREM. You did right.

ABRAHAM. On the third night after the vision, when for weariness I had fallen asleep, I saw the beast again, but now it was lying dead at my feet, and the dove was flying heavenwards safe and unhurt.

EPHREM. I am rejoiced to hear this, for to my

thinking it means that some day Mary will return to you.

ABRAHAM. I was trying to get rid of the uneasiness with which the first vision had filled me by thinking of the second, when my little pupil in her cell came to my mind. I remembered, although at the time I was not alarmed, that for two days I had not heard her chanting the divine praises.

EPHREM. You were too tardy in noticing this.

ABRAHAM. I admit it. I went at once to her cell, and, knocking at the window, I called her again and again, " Mary ! My child ! Mary ! "

EPHREM. You called in vain ?

ABRAHAM. " Mary," I said. " Mary, my child, what is wrong ? Why are you not saying your office ? " It was only when I did not hear the faintest sound that I suspected.

EPHREM. What did you do then ?

ABRAHAM. When I could no longer doubt that she had gone, I was struck with fear to my very bowels. I trembled in every limb.

EPHREM. I do not wonder, since I, hearing of it, find myself trembling all over.

ABRAHAM. Then I wept and cried out to the empty air, " What wolf has seized my lamb ? What thief has stolen my little daughter ? "

EPHREM. You had good cause to weep ! To lose her whom you had cherished so tenderly !

ABRAHAM. At last some people came up who knew what had happened. From them I learned that she had gone back to the world.

EPHREM. Where is she now?

ABRAHAM. No one knows.

EPHREM. What is to be done?

ABRAHAM. I have a faithful friend, who is searching all the cities and towns in the country. He says he will never give up until he finds her.

EPHREM. And if he finds her—what then?

ABRAHAM. Then I shall change these clothes, and in the guise of a worldling seek her out. It may be that she will heed what I say, and even after this shipwreck turn again to the harbour of her innocence and peace.

EPHREM. And suppose that in the world they offer you flesh meat and wine?

ABRAHAM. If they do, I shall not refuse; otherwise I might be recognized.

EPHREM. No one will blame you, brother. It will be but praiseworthy discretion on your part to loosen the bridle of strict observance for the sake of bringing back a soul.

ABRAHAM. I am the more eager to try now I know you approve.

EPHREM. He Who knows the secret places of the heart can tell with what motive every action is done. That scrupulous and fair Judge will not condemn a man for relaxing our strict rule for a time and descending to the level of weaker mortals if by so doing he can make more sure of rescuing an errant soul.

ABRAHAM. Help me with your prayers. Pray that I may not be caught in the snares of the devil.

EPHREM. May He Who is supreme good itself, without Whom no good thing can be done, bless your enterprise and bring it to a happy end !

SCENE IV

ABRAHAM. Can that be my friend who two years ago went to search for Mary ? Yes, it is he !

FRIEND. Good-day, venerable father.

ABRAHAM. Good-day, dear friend. I have waited so long for you. Of late I had begun to despair.

FRIEND. Forgive me, father. I delayed my return because I did not wish to mock you with doubtful and unreliable news. As soon as I had discovered the truth I lost no time.

ABRAHAM. You have seen Mary ?

FRIEND. I have seen her.

ABRAHAM. Where is she ? Come, sir, speak ! Tell me where.

FRIEND. It goes to my heart to tell you.

ABRAHAM. Speak—I implore you.

FRIEND. She lives in the house of a man who trades in the love of young girls like her. A profitable business, for every day he makes a large sum of money out of her lovers.

ABRAHAM. Her lovers ?   Mary's lovers ?

FRIEND. Yes.

ABRAHAM. Who are they ?

FRIEND. There are plenty of them.

ABRAHAM. Good Jesu, what is this monstrous thing I hear ?   Do they say that she, whom I brought up to be Thy bride, gives herself to strange lovers ?

FRIEND. It comes naturally to harlots.

ABRAHAM. If you are my friend, get me a saddle-horse somewhere and a soldier's dress.   I am going to get into that place as a lover.

FRIEND. Father, mine are at your service.

ABRAHAM. And I must borrow a felt hat to cover my tonsure.

FRIEND. That is most necessary, if you do not want to be recognized.

ABRAHAM. I have one gold piece.   Should I take it to give this man ?

FRIEND. You should, for otherwise he will never let you see Mary.

SCENE V

ABRAHAM. Good-day, friend.

INN-KEEPER. Who's   there ?   Good-day,   Sir. Come in !

ABRAHAM. Have you a bed for a traveller who wants to spend a night here ?

INN-KEEPER. Why certainly! I never turn any-one away.

ABRAHAM. I am glad of it.

INN-KEEPER. Come in then, and I will order supper for you.

ABRAHAM. I owe you thanks for this kind welcome, but I have a greater favour to ask.

INN-KEEPER. Ask what you like. I will do my best for you.

ABRAHAM. Accept this small present. May the beautiful girl who, I am told, lives here, have supper with me?

INN-KEEPER. Why should *you* wish to see her?

ABRAHAM. It would give me much pleasure. I have heard so much talk of her beauty.

INN-KEEPER. Whoever has spoken to you of her has told only the truth. It would be hard to find a finer wench.

ABRAHAM. I am in love with her already.

INN-KEEPER. It's queer that an old man like you should dangle after a young girl.

ABRAHAM. I swear I came here on purpose to feast my eyes on her.

SCENE VI

INN-KEEPER. Mary, come here! Come along now and show off your charms to this young innocent!

MARY. I am coming.

ABRAHAM. Oh, mind, be constant! Tears, do not fall! Must I look on her whom I brought up in the desert, decked out with a harlot's face? Yes, I must hide what is in my heart. I must strive not to weep, and smile though my heart is breaking.

INN-KEEPER. Luck comes your way, Mary! Not only do young gallants of your own age flock to your arms, but even the wise and venerable!

MARY. It is all one to me. It is my business to love those who love me.

ABRAHAM. Come nearer, Mary, and give me a kiss.

MARY. I will give you more than a kiss. I will take your head in my arms and stroke your neck.

ABRAHAM. Yes, like that!

MARY. What does this mean? What is this lovely fragrance. So clean, so sweet. It reminds me of the time when I was good.

ABRAHAM. On with the mask! Chatter, make lewd jests like an idle boy! She must not recognize me, or for very shame she may fly from me.

MARY. Wretch that I am! To what have I fallen! In what pit am I sunk!

ABRAHAM. You forget where you are! Do men come here to see you cry!

INN-KEEPER. What's the matter, Lady Mary? Why are you in the dumps? You have lived here two years, and never before have I seen a tear, never heard a sigh or a word of complaint.

MARY. Oh, that I had died three years ago before I came to this !

ABRAHAM. I came here to make love to you, not to weep with you over your sins.

MARY. A little thing moved me, and I spoke foolishly. It is nothing. Come, let us eat and drink and be merry, for, as you say, this is not the place to think of one's sins.

ABRAHAM. I have eaten and drunk enough, thanks to your good table, Sir. Now by your leave I will go to bed. My tired limbs need a rest.

INN-KEEPER. As you please.

MARY. Get up my lord. I will take you to bed.

ABRAHAM. I hope so. I would not go at all unless you came with me.

SCENE VII

MARY. Look ! How do you like this room ? A handsome bed, isn't it ? Those trappings cost a lot of money. Sit down and I will take off your shoes. You seem tired.

ABRAHAM. First bolt the door. Someone may come in.

MARY. Have no fear. I have seen to that.

ABRAHAM. The time has come for me to show my shaven head, and make myself known ! Oh, my daughter ! Oh, Mary, you who are part of my soul !

Look at me. Do you not know me ? Do you not know the old man who cherished you with a father's love, and wedded you to the Son of the King of Heaven ?

MARY. God, what shall I do ! It is my father and master Abraham !

ABRAHAM. What has come to you, daughter ?

MARY. Oh, misery !

ABRAHAM. Who deceived you ? Who led you astray ?

MARY. Who deceived our first parents ?

ABRAHAM. Have you forgotten that once you lived like an angel on earth !

MARY. All that is over.

ABRAHAM. What has become of your virginal modesty ? Your beautiful purity ?

MARY. Lost. Gone !

ABRAHAM. Oh, Mary, think what you have thrown away ! Think what a reward you had earned by your fasting, and prayers, and vigils. What can they avail you now ! You have hurled yourself from heavenly heights into the depths of hell !

MARY. Oh God, I know it !

ABRAHAM. Could you not trust me ? Why did you desert me ? Why did you not tell me of your fall ? Then dear brother Ephrem and I could have done a worthy penance.

MARY. Once I had committed that sin, and was defiled, how could I dare come near you who are so holy ?

ABRAHAM. Oh, Mary, has anyone ever lived on earth without sin except the Virgin's Son ?

MARY. No one, I know.

ABRAHAM. It is human to sin, but it is devilish to remain in sin. Who can be justly condemned ? Not those who fall suddenly, but those who refuse to rise quickly.

MARY. Wretched, miserable creature that I am !

ABRAHAM. Why have you thrown yourself down there ? Why do you lie on the ground without moving or speaking ? Get up, Mary ! Get up, my child, and listen to me !

MARY. No ! no ! I am afraid. I cannot bear your reproaches.

ABRAHAM. Remember how I love you, and you will not be afraid.

MARY. It is useless. I cannot.

ABRAHAM. What but love for you could have made me leave the desert and relax the strict observance of our rule ? What but love could have made me, a true hermit, come into the city and mix with the lascivious crowd ? It is for your sake that these lips have learned to utter light, foolish words, so that I might not be known ! Oh, Mary, why do you turn away your face from me and gaze upon the ground ? Why do you scorn to answer and tell me what is in your mind.

MARY. It is the thought of my sins which crushes me. I dare not look at you ; I am not fit to speak to you.

ABRAHAM. My little one, have no fear. Oh, do not despair! Rise from this abyss of desperation and grapple God to your soul!

MARY. No, no! My sins are too great. They weigh me down.

ABRAHAM. The mercy of heaven is greater than you or your sins. Let your sadness be dispersed by its glorious beams. Oh, Mary, do not let apathy prevent your seizing the moment for repentance. It matters not how wickedness has flourished. Divine grace can flourish still more abundantly!

MARY. If there were the smallest hope of forgiveness, surely I should not shrink from doing penance.

ABRAHAM. Have you no pity for me? I have sought you out with so much pain and weariness! Oh shake off this despair which we are taught is the most terrible of all sins. Despair of God's mercy—for that alone there is no forgiveness. Sin can no more embitter His sweet mercy than a spark from a flint can set the ocean on fire.

MARY. I know that God's mercy is great, but when I think how greatly I have sinned, I cannot believe any penance can make amends.

ABRAHAM. I will take your sins on me. Only come back and take up your life again as if you had never left it.

MARY. I do not want to oppose you. What you tell me to do I will do with all my heart.

ABRAHAM. My daughter lives again ! I have found my lost lamb and she is dearer to me than ever.

MARY. I have a few possessions here—a little gold and some clothes.   What ought I to do with them ?

ABRAHAM. What came to you through sin, with sin must be left behind.

MARY. Could it not be given to the poor, or sold for an offering at the holy altar ?

ABRAHAM. The price of sin is not an acceptable offering to God.

MARY. Then I will not trouble any more about my possessions.

ABRAHAM. Look ! The dawn ! It is growing light.   Let us go.

MARY. You go first, dearest father, like the good shepherd leading the lost lamb that has been found.   The lamb will follow in your steps.

ABRAHAM. Not so ! I am going on foot, but you— you shall have a horse so that the stony road shall not hurt your delicate feet.

MARY. Oh, let me never forget this tenderness ! Let me try all my life to thank you ! I was not worth pity, yet you have shown me no harshness ; you have led me to repent not by threats but by gentleness and love.

ABRAHAM. I ask only one thing, Mary.   Be faithful to God for the rest of your life.

MARY. With all my strength I will persevere, and though my flesh may fail, my spirit never will.

ABRAHAM. You must serve God with as much energy as you have served the world.

MARY. If His will is made perfect in me it will be because of your merits.

ABRAHAM. Come, let us hasten on our way.

MARY. Yes, let us set out at once. I would not stay here another moment.

SCENE VIII

ABRAHAM. Courage, Mary! You see how swiftly we have made the difficult and toilsome journey.

MARY. Everything is easy when we put our hearts into it.

ABRAHAM. There is your deserted little cell.

MARY. God help me! It was the witness of my sin. I dare not go there.

ABRAHAM. It is natural you should dread the place where the enemy triumphed.

MARY. Where, then, am I to do penance?

ABRAHAM. Go into the inner cell. There you will be safe from the wiles of the serpent.

MARY. Most gladly as it is your wish.

ABRAHAM. Now I must go to my good friend Ephrem. He alone mourned with me when you were lost, and he must rejoice with me now that you have been found.

MARY. Of course.

SCENE IX

EPHREM. Well, brother ! If I am not mistaken, you bring good news.

ABRAHAM. The best in the world.

EPHREM. You have found your lost lamb ?

ABRAHAM. I have, and, rejoicing, have brought her back to the fold.

EPHREM. Truly this is the work of divine grace.

ABRAHAM. That is certain.

EPHREM. How is she spending her days ? I should like to know how you have ordered her life. What does she do ?

ABRAHAM. All that I tell her.

EPHREM. That is well.

ABRAHAM. Nothing is too difficult for her— nothing too hard. She is ready to endure anything.

EPHREM. That is better.

ABRAHAM. She wears a hair shirt, and subdues her flesh with continual vigils and fasts. She is making the poor frail body obey the spirit by the most rigorous discipline.

EPHREM. Only through such a severe penance can the stains left by the pleasures of the flesh be washed away.

ABRAHAM. Those who hear her sobs are cut to the heart, and the tale of her repentance has turned many from their sins.

EPHREM. It is often so.

ABRAHAM. She prays continually for the men who through her were tempted to sin, and begs that she who was their ruin may be their salvation.

EPHREM. It is right that she should do this.

ABRAHAM. She strives to make her life as beautiful as for a time it was hideous.

EPHREM. I rejoice at what you tell me. To the depths of my heart.

ABRAHAM. And with us rejoice phalanxes of angels, praising the Lord for the conversion of a sinner.

EPHREM. Over whom, we are told, there is more joy in heaven than over the just man who needs no penance.

ABRAHAM. The more glory to Him, because there seemed no hope on earth that she could be saved.

EPHREM. Let us sing a song of thanksgiving—let us glorify the only begotten Son of God, Who of His love and mercy will not let them perish whom He redeemed with His holy blood.

ABRAHAM. To Him be honour, glory, and praise through infinite ages. Amen.

PAPHNUTIUS

ARGUMENT

THE conversion of Thais by the hermit Paphnutius. Obedient to a vision, he leaves the desert, and, disguised as a lover, seeks out Thais in Alexandria. She is moved to repent by his exhortations and, renouncing her evil life, consents to be enclosed in a narrow cell, where she does penance for three years. Paphnutius learns from a vision granted to Anthony's disciple Paul that her humility has won her a place among the blessed in Paradise. He brings her out of her cell and stays by her side until her soul has left her body.

CHARACTERS

PAPHNUTIUS.
THAIS.
THE ABBESS.
LOVERS OF THAIS.
DISCIPLES OF PAPHNUTIUS.
ANTONY.
PAUL.

PAPHNUTIUS

SCENE I

DISCIPLES.* Why do you look so gloomy, father Paphnutius ? Why do you not smile at us as usual ?

PAPHNUTIUS. When the heart is sad the face clouds over. It is only natural.

DISCIPLES. But why are you sad ?

PAPHNUTIUS. I grieve over an injury to my Creator.

DISCIPLES. What injury ?

PAPHNUTIUS. The injury His own creatures made in His very image inflict on Him.

DISCIPLES. Oh, father, your words fill us with fear ! How can such things be ?

PAPHNUTIUS. It is true that the impassible Majesty cannot be hurt by injuries. Nevertheless, speaking in metaphor, and as if God were weak with our weakness, what greater injury can we conceive than this —that while the greater world is obedient, and subject to His rule, the lesser world resists His guidance ?

* When *Paphnutius* was acted, the dialogue of the " disciples " was allotted to several different actors, with the interesting result that some definite characters emerged.

DISCIPLES. What do you mean by the lesser world ?

PAPHNUTIUS. Man.

DISCIPLES. Man ?

PAPHNUTIUS. Yes.

DISCIPLES. What man ?

PAPHNUTIUS. Every man.

DISCIPLES. How can this be ?

PAPHNUTIUS. It has pleased our Creator.

DISCIPLES. We do not understand.

PAPHNUTIUS. It is not plain to many.

DISCIPLES. Explain, father.

PAPHNUTIUS. Be attentive, then.

DISCIPLES. We are eager to learn.

PAPHNUTIUS. You know that the greater world is composed of four elements which are contraries, yet by the will of the Creator these contraries are adjusted in harmonious arrangement. Now, man is composed of even more contrary parts.

DISCIPLES. What can be more contrary than the elements ?

PAPHNUTIUS. The body and the soul. The soul is not mortal like the body, nor the body spiritual as is the soul.

DISCIPLES. That is true. But what did you mean, father, when you spoke of " harmonious arrangement " ?

PAPHNUTIUS. I meant that as low and high sounds harmoniously united produce a certain music, so discordant elements rightly adjusted make one world.

DISCIPLES. It seems strange that discords can become concords.

PAPHNUTIUS. Consider. No thing is composed of " likes "—neither can it be made up of elements which have no proportion among themselves, or which are entirely different in substance and nature.

DISCIPLES. What is music, master ?

PAPHNUTIUS. One of the branches of the " quadrivium " of philosophy, my son. Arithmetic, geometry, music, and philosophy form the quadrivium.

DISCIPLES. I should like to know why they are given that name.

PAPHNUTIUS. Because just as paths branch out from the quadrivium, the place where four roads meet, so do these subjects lead like roads from one principle of philosophy.

DISCIPLES. We had best not question you about the other three, for our slow wits can scarcely follow what you have told us about the first.

PAPHNUTIUS. It is a difficult subject.

DISCIPLES. Still you might give us a general idea of the nature of music.

PAPHNUTIUS. It is hard to explain to hermits to whom it is an unknown science.

DISCIPLES. Is there more than one kind of music ?

PAPHNUTIUS. There are three kinds, my son. The first is celestial, the second human, the third is produced by instruments.

DISCIPLES. In what does the celestial consist ?

PAPHNUTIUS. In the seven planets and the celestial globe.

DISCIPLES. But how ?

PAPHNUTIUS. Exactly as in instruments. You find the same number of intervals of the same length, and the same concords as in strings.

DISCIPLES. We do not understand what intervals are.

PAPHNUTIUS. The dimensions which are reckoned between planets or between notes.

DISCIPLES. And what are their lengths ?

PAPHNUTIUS. The same as tones.

DISCIPLES. We are none the wiser.

PAPHNUTIUS. A tone is composed of two sounds, and bears the ratio of nine to eight.

DISCIPLES. As soon as we get over one difficulty, you place a greater one in our path !

PAPHNUTIUS. That is inevitable in a discussion of this kind.

DISCIPLES. Yet tell us something about concord, so that at least we may know the meaning of the word.

PAPHNUTIUS. Concord, harmony, or symphonia may be defined as a fitting disposition of modulation. It is composed sometimes of three, sometimes of four, sometimes of five sounds.

DISCIPLES. As you have given us these three distinctions, we should like to learn the name of each.

PAPHNUTIUS. The first is called a fourth, as consisting of four sounds, and it has the proportion of four to three. The second is called a fifth. It consists of five sounds and bears the ratio of one and a half. The third is known as the diapason; it is double and is perfected in eight sounds.

DISCIPLES. And do the spheres and planets produce sounds, since they are compared to notes?

PAPHNUTIUS. Undoubtedly they do.

DISCIPLE. Why is the music not heard?

DISCIPLES. Yes, why is it not heard?

PAPHNUTIUS. Many reasons are given. Some think it is not heard because it is so continuous that men have grown accustomed to it. Others say it is because of the density of the air. Some assert that so enormous a sound could not pass into the mortal ear. Others that the music of the spheres is so pleasant and sweet that if it were heard all men would come together, and, forgetting themselves and all their pursuits, would follow the sounds from east to west.

DISCIPLES. It is well that it is not heard.

PAPHNUTIUS. As our Creator foreknew.

DISCIPLES. We have heard enough of this kind of music. What of " human " music?

PAPHNUTIUS. What do you want to know about that?

DISCIPLES. How is it manifested?

PAPHNUTIUS. Not only, as I have already told you,

in the combination of body and soul, and in the utterance of the voice, now high, now low, but even in the pulsation of the veins, and in the proportion of our members. Take the finger-joints. In them, if we measure, we find the same proportions as we have already found in concord; for music is said to be a fitting disposition not only of sounds, but of things with no resemblance to sounds.

DISCIPLES. Had we known the difficulty that such a hard point presents to the ignorant, we would not have asked you about your " lesser world." It is better to know nothing than to be bewildered.

PAPHNUTIUS. I do not agree. By trying to understand you have learned many things that you did not know before.

DISCIPLES. That is true.

DISCIPLE. True it may be, but I am weary of this disputation. We are all weary, because we cannot follow the reasoning of such a philosopher !

PAPHNUTIUS. Why do you laugh at me, children ? I am no philosopher, but an ignorant man.

DISCIPLES. Where did you get all this learning with which you have puzzled our heads ?

PAPHNUTIUS. It is but a little drop from the full deep wells of learning—wells at which I, a chance passer-by, have lapped, but never sat down to drain.

DISCIPLE. We are grateful for your patience with us ; but I for one cannot forget the warning of the

Apostle : " God hath chosen the foolish things of the world to confound the wise."

PAPHNUTIUS. Whether a fool or a wise man does wrong, he will be confounded.

DISCIPLES. True.

PAPHNUTIUS. Nor is God offended by Knowledge of the Knowable, only by undue pride on the part of the Knower.

DISCIPLES. That is well said.

PAPHNUTIUS. And I would ask you—unto whose praise can the knowledge of the arts be more worthily or more justly turned than to the praise of Him Who made things capable of being known, and gave us the capacity to know them ?

DISCIPLES. Truly, to none.

PAPHNUTIUS. The more a man realizes the wonderful way in which God has set all things in number and measure and weight, the more ardent his love.

DISCIPLES. That is as it should be.

PAPHNUTIUS. But I am wrong to dwell on matters which give you so little pleasure.

DISCIPLES. Tell us the cause of your sadness. Relieve us of the burden of our curiosity.

PAPHNUTIUS. Perhaps you will not find the tale to your liking.

DISCIPLES. A man is often sadder for having his curiosity satisfied, yet he cannot overcome this tendency to be curious. It is part of our weakness.

PAPHNUTIUS. Brothers—there is a woman, a shameless woman, living in our neighbourhood.

DISCIPLES. A perilous thing for the people.

PAPHNUTIUS. Her beauty is wonderful: her impurity is—horrible.

DISCIPLES. What is her wretched name?

PAPHNUTIUS. Thais.

DISCIPLES. Thais! Thais, the harlot!

PAPHNUTIUS. Yes—she.

DISCIPLE. Everyone has heard of her and her wickedness.

PAPHNUTIUS. It is no wonder, for she is not satisfied to ruin herself with a small band of lovers. She seeks to allure all men through her marvellous beauty, and drag them down with her.

DISCIPLES. What a woeful thing!

PAPHNUTIUS. And it is not only fools and wastrels who squander their substance with her. Citizens of high standing and virtue lay precious things at her feet, and enrich her to their own undoing.

DISCIPLES. It is terrible to hear of such things.

PAPHNUTIUS. Flocks of lovers crowd to her doors.

DISCIPLES. And to their destruction!

PAPHNUTIUS. They are so crazed with desire that they quarrel and fight for admission to her house.

DISCIPLES. One vice brings another in its train.

PAPHNUTIUS. They come to blows. Heads are

broken, faces bruised, noses smashed ; at times they drive each other out with weapons, and the threshold of the vile place is dyed with blood !

DISCIPLES. Most horrible !

PAPHNUTIUS. This is the injury to the Creator for which I weep day and night. This is the cause of my sorrow.

DISCIPLES. We understand now. You have good reason to be distressed, and I doubt not that the citizens of the heavenly country share your grief.

PAPHNUTIUS. Oh, to rescue her from that wicked life ! Why should I not try ?

DISCIPLES. God forbid !

PAPHNUTIUS. Brother, our Lord Jesus went among sinners.

DISCIPLES. She would not receive a hermit.

PAPHNUTIUS. What if I were to go in the disguise of a lover ?

DISCIPLE. If that thought is from God, God will give you strength to accomplish it.

PAPHNUTIUS. I will set out immediately. I shall need your best prayers. Pray that I may not be overcome by the wiles of the serpent. Pray that I may be able to show this soul the beauty of divine love.

DISCIPLE. May He Who laid low the Prince of Darkness give you the victory over the enemy of the human race.

SCENE II

PAPHNUTIUS. I am bewildered in this town. I cannot find my way. Now I shut my eyes, and I am back in the desert. I can hear my children's voices praising God. Good children, I know you are praying for me ! I fear to speak. I fear to ask my way. O God, come to my help ! I see some young men in the market-place. They are coming this way. I will go up to them and ask where she is to be found.

THE YOUNG MEN. That stranger seems to want to speak to us.

YOUNG MAN. Let us go and find out.

PAPHNUTIUS. Your pardon, gentlemen. Am I speaking to citizens of this town ?

YOUNG MAN. You are. Can we do anything for you ?

PAPHNUTIUS. My salutations !

YOUNG MAN. And ours, whether you are a native or a foreigner.

PAPHNUTIUS. I am a stranger.

YOUNG MAN. What brings you here ? Have you come for pleasure, business, or learning ? This is a great city for learning. Which is it ?

PAPHNUTIUS. I cannot say.

YOUNG MAN. Why ?

PAPHNUTIUS. That is my secret.

YOUNG MAN. It would be wiser to tell us your

secret. It will be difficult for you, a stranger, to do your business here without the advice of us citizens.

PAPHNUTIUS. But if I tell you, you may try to hinder me from carrying out my plans.

YOUNG MAN. You can trust us. We are men of honour!

PAPHNUTIUS. I believe it. I will trust in your loyalty and tell you my secret.

YOUNG MAN. We are not traitors. No harm shall come to you.

PAPHNUTIUS. I am told that there lives in this town a woman who loves all who love her. She is kind to all men; she'll not deny them anything.

YOUNG MAN. Stranger, you must tell us her name. There are many women of that kind in our city. Do you know her name?

PAPHNUTIUS. Yes, I know it.

YOUNG MAN. Who is she?

PAPHNUTIUS. Thais.

YOUNG MAN. Thais! She is the flame of this land! She sets all hearts on fire.

PAPHNUTIUS. They say she is beautiful. The most exquisite woman of her kind in the world!

YOUNG MAN. They have not deceived you.

PAPHNUTIUS. For her sake I have made a long and difficult journey. I have come here only to see her.

YOUNG MAN. Well, what should prevent you? You are young and handsome.

PAPHNUTIUS. Where does she live ?

YOUNG MAN. Over there.   Her house is quite near this place.

PAPHNUTIUS. That house ?

YOUNG MAN. Yes, to the left of the statue.

PAPHNUTIUS. I will go there.

YOUNG MAN. If you like, we will come with you.

PAPHNUTIUS. I thank you for the courtesy, but I would rather go alone.

YOUNG MAN. We understand.   Have you money in your purse, stranger ?   Thais loves a handsome face, but she loves a full purse more.

PAPHNUTIUS. Gentlemen, I am rich.   I have a rare present to offer her.

YOUNG MAN. To our next meeting, then ! Farewell.   May Thais be kind !

PAPHNUTIUS. Farewell.

SCENE III

PAPHNUTIUS. Thais !   Thais !

THAIS. Who is there ?   I do not know that voice.

PAPHNUTIUS. Thais !   Your   lover   speaks ! Thais !

THAIS. Stranger, who are you ?

PAPHNUTIUS. Arise, my love, my beautiful one, and come !

THAIS. Who are you ?

PAPHNUTIUS. A man who loves you !

THAIS. And what do you want with me?

PAPHNUTIUS. I will show you.

THAIS. You would be my lover?

PAPHNUTIUS. I am your lover, Thais, flame of the world!

THAIS. Whoever loves me is well paid. He receives as much as he gives.

PAPHNUTIUS. Oh, Thais, Thais! If you knew what a long and troublesome journey I have come to speak to you—to see your face!

THAIS. Well? Have I refused to speak to you, or to show you my face?

PAPHNUTIUS. I cannot speak to you here. I must be with you alone. What I have to say is secret. The room must be secret too.

THAIS. How would you like a bedchamber, fragrant with perfumes, adorned as for a marriage? I have such a room. Look!

PAPHNUTIUS. Is there no room still more secret—a room that your lovers do not know? Some room where you and I might hide from all the world?

THAIS. Yes, there is a room like that in this house. No one even knows that it exists except myself, and God.

PAPHNUTIUS. God! What God?

THAIS. The true God.

PAPHNUTIUS. You believe that He exists?

THAIS. I am a Christian.

PAPHNUTIUS. And you believe that He knows what we do ?

THAIS. I believe He knows everything.

PAPHNUTIUS. What do you think, then ? That He is indifferent to the actions of the sinner, or that He reserves judgment ?

THAIS. I suppose that the merits of each man are weighed in the balance, and that we shall be punished or rewarded according to our deeds.

PAPHNUTIUS. O Christ ! How wondrous is Thy patience ! How wondrous is Thy love ! Even when those who believe in Thee sin deliberately, Thou dost delay their destruction !

THAIS. Why do you tremble ? Why do you turn pale ? Why do you weep ?

PAPHNUTIUS. I shudder at your presumption. I weep for your damnation. How, knowing what you know, can you destroy men in this manner and ruin so many souls, all precious and immortal ?

THAIS. Your voice pierces my heart ! Strange lover—you are cruel. Pity me !

PAPHNUTIUS. Let us pity rather those souls whom you have deprived of the sight of God— of the God Whom you confess ! Oh, Thais, you have wilfully offended the divine Majesty. That condemns you.

THAIS. What do you mean ? Why do you threaten me like this ?

PAPHNUTIUS. Because the punishment of hell-fire awaits you if you remain in sin.

THAIS. Who are you, who rebuke me so sternly? Oh, you have shaken me to the depths of my terrified heart!

PAPHNUTIUS. I would that you could be shaken with fear to your very bowels! I would like to see your delicate body impregnated with terror in every vein, and every fibre, if that would keep you from yielding to the dangerous delights of the flesh.

THAIS. And what zest for pleasure do you think is left now in a heart suddenly awakened to a consciousness of guilt! Remorse has killed everything.

PAPHNUTIUS. I long to see the thorns of vice cut away, and the choked-up fountain of your tears flowing once more. Tears of repentance are precious in the sight of God.

THAIS. Oh, voice that promises mercy! Do you believe, can you hope that one so vile as I, soiled by thousands and thousands of impurities, can make reparation, can ever by any manner of penance obtain pardon?

PAPHNUTIUS. Thais, no sin is so great, no crime so black, that it cannot be expiated by tears and penitence, provided they are followed up by deeds.

THAIS. Show me, I beg you, my father, what I can do to be reconciled with Him I have offended.

PAPHNUTIUS. Despise the world. Leave your dissolute lovers.

THAIS. And afterwards? What then?

PAPHNUTIUS. You must retire to some solitary place, where you may learn to know yourself and realize the enormity of your sins.

THAIS. If you think this will save me, I will not delay a moment.

PAPHNUTIUS. I have no doubt it will.

THAIS. Yet give me a little time. I must collect the wealth that I have gained through the sins of my body— all the treasures I have kept too long.

PAPHNUTIUS. Do not give them a moment's thought. There will be no lack of people to find them and make use of them.

THAIS. I have another idea in my mind. I did not think of keeping this wealth or of giving it to my friends. Nor would I distribute it among the poor. The wages of sin are no material for good works.

PAPHNUTIUS. You are right. What then do you propose to do with your possessions?

THAIS. Give them to the flames! Burn them to ashes!

PAPHNUTIUS. For what reason?

THAIS. That they may no longer exist in the world. Each one was acquired at the cost of an injury to the goodness and beauty of the Creator. Let them burn.

PAPHNUTIUS. How you are changed ! Grace is on your lips ! Your eyes are calm, and impure passions no longer burn in them. Oh, miracle ! Is this Thais who was once so greedy for gold ? Is this Thais, who seeks so humbly the feet of God ?

THAIS. God give me grace to change still more. My heart is changed, but this mortal substance—how shall it be changed ?

PAPHNUTIUS. It is not difficult for the unchangeable substance to transform us.

THAIS. Now I am going to carry out my plan. Fire shall destroy everything I have.

PAPHNUTIUS. Go in peace. Then return to me here quickly. Do not delay ! I trust your resolution, and yet——

THAIS. You need not be afraid.

PAPHNUTIUS. Thais, come back quickly ! God be with you !

SCENE IV

THAIS. Come, my lovers ! Come, all my evil lovers ! Hasten, my lovers ! Your Thais calls you !

LOVERS. That is the voice of Thais. She calls us. Let us make haste. Let us make haste, for by delay we may offend her.

THAIS. Come, lovers ! Run ! Hasten ! What makes you so slow ? Never has Thais been more impatient for your coming. Come nearer. I have something to tell you all.

LOVERS. Oh, Thais, what is the meaning of this pile of faggots? Why are you throwing all those beautiful and precious treasures on the pile?

THAIS. You cannot guess? You do not know why I have built this fire?

LOVERS. We are amazed. We wonder greatly what is the meaning of it and of your strange looks.

THAIS. You would like me to tell you, evil lovers?

LOVERS. We long to hear.

THAIS. Look, then!

LOVERS. Stop, Thais! What are you doing? Are you mad?

THAIS. I am not mad. For the first time I am sane, and I rejoice!

LOVERS. To waste these pounds of gold, and all the other treasure! Oh, Thais, you have lost your senses! These are beautiful things, precious things, and you burn them!

THAIS. All these things I have extorted from you as the price of shameful deeds. I burn them to destroy all hope in you that I shall ever again turn to your love. And now I leave you.

LOVERS. Wait, Thais. Oh wait a little, and tell us what has changed you!

THAIS. I will not stay. I will not tell you anything. To talk with you has become loathsome.

LOVERS. What have we done to deserve this scorn and contempt? Can you accuse us of being unfaithful? What wrong have we done? We have always sought to satisfy your desires. And now you show us this bitter hatred! Unjust woman, what have we done?

THAIS. Leave me, or let me leave you. Do not touch me. You can tear my garments, but you shall not touch me.

LOVERS. Cruel Thais, speak to us! Before you go, speak to us!

THAIS. I have sinned with you. But now is the end of sin, and all our wild pleasures are ended.

LOVERS. Thais, do not leave us! Thais, where are you going?

THAIS. Where none of you will ever see me again!

LOVERS. What monstrous thing is this? Thais, glory of our land, is changed! Thais, our delight, who loved riches and power and luxury—Thais, who gave herself up to pleasure day and night, has destroyed past remedy gold and gems that had no price! What monstrous thing is this? Thais, the very flower of love, insults her lovers and scorns their gifts. Thais, whose boast it was that whoever loved her should enjoy her love! What monstrous thing is this? Thais! Thais! this is a thing not to be believed.

SCENE V

THAIS. Paphnutius, my father, I am ready now to obey you, command what you will.

PAPHNUTIUS. Thais, I have been uneasy during your absence. I feared you had been caught in the world's snare. I feared you would not return.

THAIS. You need not have been afraid. The world does not tempt me now. My possessions are ashes. I have publicly renounced my lovers.

PAPHNUTIUS. Oh, happy guilt that has brought such happy penitence! Since you have renounced your earthly lovers, you can now be joined to your Heavenly Lover.

THAIS. It is for you to show me the way. Be a lantern to me, for all is obscure night.

PAPHNUTIUS. Trust me, daughter.   Follow me.

THAIS. I can follow you with my feet. Would that I could follow you with my deeds!

SCENE VI

THAIS. Oh, I am weary!

PAPHNUTIUS. Courage! Here is the monastery where a famous community of holy virgins live. I am anxious for you to pass the time of penance here if you will consent.

THAIS. I do not resist.   I wish to obey you.   I trust
you.

PAPHNUTIUS. I will go in, and persuade the
Abbess who is the head of the community to receive
you.

THAIS. And what shall I do meanwhile ?   Do not
leave me alone.

PAPHNUTIUS. You shall come with me. But
look ! The Abbess has come out to meet us. I wonder
who can have told her so promptly of our arrival.

THAIS. Rumour, Father Paphnutius.   Rumour
never delays.

SCENE VII

PAPHNUTIUS. You come opportunely, illustrious
Abbess.   I was just seeking you.

ABBESS. You are most welcome, venerated Father
Paphnutius. Blessed is your visit, beloved of the Most
High.

PAPHNUTIUS. May the grace of Him Who is
Father of all pour into your heart the beatitude of everlasting peace !

ABBESS. And what has brought your holiness to my
humble dwelling ?

PAPHNUTIUS. I need your help.

ABBESS. Speak but the word. You will find me eager
to do all in my power to carry out your wishes.

PAPHNUTIUS. Oh, Abbess, I have brought you a little wild gazelle who has been snatched half dead from the jaws of wolves. Show it compassion, nurse it with all your tenderness, until it has shed its rough goatskin and put on the soft fleece of a lamb.

ABBESS. Explain yourself further.

PAPHNUTIUS. You see this woman. From her youth she has led the life of a harlot. She has given herself up to base pleasures——

ABBESS. What misery !

PAPHNUTIUS. She cannot offer the excuse that she was a Pagan to whom such pleasures bring no remorse of conscience. She wore the baptismal robes of a child of God when she gave herself to the flames of profane love. She was not tempted. She chose this evil life. She was ruined by her own will.

ABBESS. She is the more unfortunate.

PAPHNUTIUS. Yet such is the power of Christ, that at His word, of which my poor mouth was the instrument, she has fled from the surroundings which were her damnation. Obedient as a child, she has followed me. She has abandoned lust and ease and idle luxury. She is resolved to live chastely.

ABBESS. Glory to the Author of the marvellous change !

PAPHNUTIUS. Amen. But since the maladies of the soul, like those of the body, need physic for their cure, we must minister to this soul diseased by years of lust. It must be removed from the foul breath of the world. A narrow cell, solitude, silence—these must be her lot henceforth. She must learn to know herself and her sins.

ABBESS. You are right. Such a penance is necessary.

PAPHNUTIUS. Will you give orders for a little cell to be made ready as soon as possible ?

ABBESS. Yes, my father. It shall be done as quickly as we can.

PAPHNUTIUS. There must be no entrance, no opening of any kind, except a small window through which she can receive the food that will be brought her on certain days at certain fixed hours. A pound of bread, and water according to her need.

ABBESS. Forgive me, dear father in God, but I fear she will not be able to endure such a rigorous life. The soul may be willing, but that fastidious mind, that delicate body used to luxury, how can we expect them to submit ?

PAPHNUTIUS. Have no fear. We know that grave sin demands a grave remedy.

ABBESS. That is true, yet are we not told also to hasten slowly ?

PAPHNUTIUS. Good mother, I am already weary of delay. What if her lovers should pursue her ? What

if she be drawn back into the abyss ? I am impatient to
see her enclosed.

ABBESS. Nothing stands in the way of your enclosing
her now. The cell which you told us to prepare is
ready.

PAPHNUTIUS. Then enter, Thais ! This is just
such a refuge as we spoke of on our journey. It is the
very place for you. There is room and more than room
here for you to weep over your sins.

THAIS. How small it is ! How dark ! How can a
delicate woman live in such a place ?

PAPHNUTIUS. You are not pleased with your new
dwelling ! You shudder at the thought of entering !
Oh, Thais, have you not wandered long enough without
restraint ? Is it not right that you should now be con-
fined in this narrow, solitary cell, where you will find
true freedom ?

THAIS. I have been so long accustomed to pleasure
and distraction. My mind is still a slave to the
senses.

PAPHNUTIUS. The more need to rein it, to discipline it, until it ceases to rebel.

THAIS. I do not rebel—but my weakness revolts
against one thing here.

PAPHNUTIUS. Of what do you speak ?

THAIS. I am ashamed to say.

PAPHNUTIUS. Speak, Thais ! Be ashamed of
nothing but your sins.

THAIS. Good father, what could be more repugnant than to have to attend to all the needs of the body in this one little room. . . . It will soon be uninhabitable.

PAPHNUTIUS. Fear the cruel punishments of the soul, and cease to dread transitory evils.

THAIS. My weakness makes me shudder.

PAPHNUTIUS. The sweetness of your guilty pleasures was far more bitter and foul.

THAIS. I know it is just. What grieves me most is that I shall not have one clean sweet spot in which to call upon the sweet name of God.

PAPHNUTIUS. Have a care, Thais, or your confidence may become presumption. Should polluted lips utter so easily the name of the unpolluted Godhead ?

THAIS. Oh, how can I hope for pardon ! Who will pity me—who save me ! What shall I do if I am forbidden to invoke Him against Whom only I have sinned ! To whom should I pray if not to Him.

PAPHNUTIUS. You must indeed pray to Him, but with tears, not with words. Let not a tinkling voice, but the mighty roar of a contrite heart sound in the ear of God.

THAIS. I desire His pardon. Surely I may ask for it ?

PAPHNUTIUS. Oh, Thais, the more perfectly you humble yourself, the more swiftly you will win it ! Let your heart be all prayer, but let your lips say only this : " O God Who made me, pity me ! "

THAIS. O God, Who made me, pity me ! He alone can save me from defeat in this hard struggle !

PAPHNUTIUS. Fight manfully, and you will gain a glorious victory.

THAIS. It is your part to pray for me ! Pray I may earn the victor's palm.

PAPHNUTIUS. You need not remind me.

THAIS. Give me some hope !

PAPHNUTIUS. Courage ! The palm will soon be in this humble hand. It is time for me to return to the desert. I owe a duty to my dear disciples. I know their hearts are torn by my absence. Yes, I must go. Venerable Abbess, I trust this captive to your charity and tenderness. I beg you to take the best care of her. Sustain her delicate body with necessaries. Refresh her soul with the luxuries of divine knowledge.

ABBESS. Have no anxiety about her, for I will cherish her with a mother's love and tenderness.

PAPHNUTIUS. I go then.

ABBESS. In peace.

SCENE VIII

DISCIPLES. Who knocks there ?

PAPHNUTIUS. It is I—your father.

DISCIPLES. It is the voice of our father Paphnutius !

PAPHNUTIUS. Unbolt the door.

DISCIPLE. Good father, welcome.

ALL. Welcome, father ! Welcome !

PAPHNUTIUS. A blessing on you all !

DISCIPLE. You have given us great uneasiness by your long absence.

PAPHNUTIUS. It has been fruitful.

DISCIPLE. Your mission has succeeded ? Come, tell us what has happened to Thais.

PAPHNUTIUS. All that I wished.

DISCIPLE. She has abandoned her evil life ?

PAPHNUTIUS. Yes.

DISCIPLE. Where is she living now ?

PAPHNUTIUS. She weeps over her sins in a little cell.

DISCIPLES. Praise be to the Supreme Trinity !

PAPHNUTIUS. A little narrow cell, no wider than a grave. Blessed be His Terrible Name now and for ever.

DISCIPLES. Amen.

SCENE IX

PAPHNUTIUS. Three years of her penance are over, and I cannot tell whether her sorrow has found favour with God. For some reason He will not enlighten me. I know what I will do. I will go to my brother Antony and beg him to intercede for me. God will make the truth known to him.

SCENE X

ANTONY. Who comes this way ?   By his dress it is some brother-dweller in the desert.   My old eyes do not recognize you yet, friend.   Come nearer.

PAPHNUTIUS. Brother Antony ! Do you not know me ?

ANTONY. This is joy indeed ! What pleasures God sends us, when we resign ourselves to have none ! I did not think to see my brother Paphnutius again in this world.   Is it indeed you, brother ?

PAPHNUTIUS. Yes, it is I.

ANTONY. You are welcome, very welcome. Your coming gives me great joy.

PAPHNUTIUS. I am no less rejoiced to see you.

ANTONY. But what is the cause ? What has brought Paphnutius from his solitary retreat ?   He is not sick, I trust ?   He has not come to old Antony for healing ?

PAPHNUTIUS. No, I am in good health.

ANTONY. That's well !   I am glad of it.

PAPHNUTIUS. Brother Antony, it is three years since my peace was broken and disturbed by the persistent vision of a soul in peril. I heard a voice calling me night and day. But I stopped my ears—fearing my weakness. I thought " She calls me to ruin me." " No, no," the voice said. " I call you to save me."

ANTONY. A woman's voice !

PAPHNUTIUS. Before my vision it was well known to us all that in the great town on the edge of the desert there was a harlot called Thais, through whom many were destroyed body and soul.

ANTONY. It was she who called you!

PAPHNUTIUS. Brother Antony, it was God who called me. My disciples opposed me; nevertheless I went to the town to see Thais and wrestle with the demon.

ANTONY. A perilous enterprise.

PAPHNUTIUS. I went to her in the disguise of a lover, and began by flattering her with sweet words. Then I threw off the mask and brought terror to her soul with bitter reproaches and threats of God's punishment.

ANTONY. A prudent course. Hard words are necessary when natures have grown soft and can no longer distinguish between good and evil.

PAPHNUTIUS. I was disarmed by her docility. Truly, brother Antony, my heart melted like wax when she spurned her ill-gotten wealth and abandoned her lovers.

ANTONY. But you hid your tenderness?

PAPHNUTIUS. Yes, Brother Antony.

ANTONY. What followed?

PAPHNUTIUS. She chose to live in chastity. She consented to be enclosed in a narrow cell. She accepted her penance with sweetness and humility.

ANTONY. I am rejoiced by what you have told me! All the blood in my old veins exults and rejoices!

PAPHNUTIUS. That is because you are a saint.

ANTONY. Brother, you cannot mean that you are sad ?

PAPHNUTIUS. I rejoice immeasurably in her conversion. Yet at times I am uneasy. I fear that the penance may have been too long and severe for a woman of such delicate frame.

ANTONY. That does you no wrong. Where true love is, loving compassion is not wanting.

PAPHNUTIUS. I came to beg yours for Thais. Of your charity give me your prayers. I beg you and your disciples to join with me in praying for a sign. Let us persevere in prayer until it is shown us from heaven that the penitent's tears have moved the divine mercy to indulgence.

ANTONY. Brother Paphnutius, I have never granted a request more gladly. Come, we will gather together my disciples.

PAPHNUTIUS. I know that God will listen to his good servant Antony.

SCENE XI

ANTONY. Thanks be to God ! The gospel's promise is fulfilled in us !

PAPHNUTIUS. What promise, blessed Antony ?

ANTONY. Those who unite in prayer can obtain whatever they desire.

PAPHNUTIUS. What miracle has happened?
What is it?

ANTONY. My disciple Paul has had a vision.

PAPHNUTIUS. What vision?   Oh, call him!

ANTONY. He is here.   Paul, my son, tell our
brother, Paphnutius, the wonders you have seen.

PAUL. Father, I saw in my vision a splendid bed.
It was adorned with white hangings and coverings, and
a crown was laid on it, and round it were four radiant
virgins.   They stood there as if they were guarding the
crown.   There was a great brightness round the bed,
and a multitude of angels.   I, seeing this wonderful and
joyful sight, cried out, " This glory must be for my master
and father Antony ! "

ANTONY. Son, did you not know Antony was
unworthy of such honour?

PAUL. But a divine voice answered me, saying,
" This glory is prepared, not, as you think, for Antony,
but for the harlot, Thais ! "

PAPHNUTIUS. O sweet Christ ! How shall I praise
Thee for so lovingly sending comfort to my sad heart?

ANTONY. He is worthy to be praised.

PAPHNUTIUS. Then farewell, Brother Antony.
I must go at once to my captive.

ANTONY. You must indeed.   It is time her valiant
penance ended.   You should assure her that her pardon
is complete ; you should fill her with hope, and speak
to her only of the beatitude in store for her.

PAPHNUTIUS. Your blessing.

SCENE XII

PAPHNUTIUS. Thais, my little daughter ! Thais !
Open the window and let me see you.

THAIS. Who speaks ?

PAPHNUTIUS. Paphnutius.

THAIS. Why should you visit a poor sinner ?   Why
should I be given this great joy and happiness ?

PAPHNUTIUS. These years that I have been absent
from you in the body have been weary to me too.   I have
thought of you night and day.   I have yearned for your
salvation.

THAIS. I never doubted that.

PAPHNUTIUS. Tell me how things are with you.
How have you lived here ?   What have you been doing ?

THAIS. Nothing worth the telling !   I have nothing
to offer God.

PAPHNUTIUS. The offering He loves best is a
humble spirit.

THAIS. All I have done is to gather up the many sins
on my conscience into a mighty bundle and keep them
always in mind.   All day I have sat gazing towards the
East, saying only this one prayer : " O God Who made
me, pity me ! "   If my bodily senses have always been
conscious of the offensiveness of this place, my heart's
eyes have never been blind to the dreadfulness of hell.

PAPHNUTIUS. Your great penitence has won a great forgiveness. Yet God has not pardoned you for your valiant expiation so much as for the love with which you have given yourself to Christ.

THAIS. Can that be true? Would that it were!

PAPHNUTIUS. Give me your hand. Let me bring you out of your cell to prove you are forgiven.

THAIS. No, father, leave me here. This place with all its uncleanness is best for me.

PAPHNUTIUS. The time has come for you to cast away your fear, and hope for life! God wishes your penance to end.

THAIS. Let the angels praise Him! He has not despised the love of a humble sinner.

PAPHNUTIUS. Thais, would you rejoice if now you were called upon to lay aside this body?

THAIS. Oh, father, my soul longs to escape from this earth.

PAPHNUTIUS. Thais, you have finished your course here. In fifteen days you will, by God's grace, pass straight to Paradise.

THAIS. To Paradise! I should be happy if I might be spared hell's torments and be mercifully cleansed in a gentle fire until my spirit is fit for the eternal happiness.

PAPHNUTIUS. Grace is the free gift of God and does not depend on our merits. If it did, it could not be called grace.

THAIS. For this let the choirs of heaven praise Him, and all the little twigs and fresh green leaves on earth, all animals, and the great waters. He is patient with us when we fall! He is generous in His gifts when we repent.

PAPHNUTIUS. He loves to be merciful. From all eternity He has preferred pardon to punishment.

SCENE XIII

THAIS. Holy father, do not leave me. Be near to comfort me in this hour of my death.

PAPHNUTIUS. I will not leave you, Thais, until your soul has taken flight to the stars, and I have buried your body.

THAIS. I feel the end is near. Brother, do not leave me!

PAPHNUTIUS. Now is the time to pray.

THAIS. O God Who made me, pity me! Grant that the soul which Thou didst breathe into me may now happily return to Thee. O God Who made me, pity me!

PAPHNUTIUS. Thais! Thais! Oh, loving humble spirit, pass to thy glory! . . . Angels lead her into Paradise! . . . O uncreated Beauty, existing in Truth without material form, grant that the divers parts of this human body now to be dissolved may return to their original elements! Grant that the soul, given from on high, may soar into light and joy, and that the body may be cherished peacefully in the soft lap of the earth until that day when, the ashes being brought together again, and the life-giving sap restored to the veins, this same Thais may rise again, a perfect human being as before, and take her place among the glorious white flock who shall be led into the joy of eternity! Grant this, O Thou Who alone art what Thou art—Who livest and reignest and art glorious in the Unity and perfect Trinity through infinite ages!

SAPIENTIA

ARGUMENT

THE martyrdom of the holy virgins Faith, Hope, and
Charity, who are put to the torture by the Emperor
Hadrian and slain in the presence of their mother
Sapientia, she encouraging them by her admonitions to
bear their sufferings. After their death the holy mother
recovers the bodies of her children, embalms them with
spices, and buries them with honour about five miles
outside the city of Rome.

Forty days later the spirit of Sapientia takes its flight
to heaven while she is still praying by her children's
graves.

CHARACTERS

ANTIOCHUS.
HADRIAN.
SAPIENTIA.
FAITH.
HOPE.
CHARITY.
MATRONS.

SAPIENTIA

SCENE I

ANTIOCHUS. My Lord Emperor, what desire has your servant but to see you powerful and prosperous? What ambition apart from the welfare and peace and greatness of the state you rule? So when I discover anything that threatens the commonwealth or your peace of mind I try to crush it before it has taken root.

HADRIAN. In this you show discretion, Antiochus. Our prosperity means your advantage. Witness the honours that we never tire of heaping on you.

ANTIOCHUS. Your Grace's welfare is so dear to me that I do not seek to disguise what is hostile to your interests, but immediately bring it to your notice and denounce it!

HADRIAN. Do you praise yourself for this? If you withheld such information you would be guilty of treason to our Imperial Majesty.

ANTIOCHUS. I have never been disloyal.

HADRIAN. I do not question it. Come, if you have discovered some new danger, make it known to us.

ANTIOCHUS. A certain alien woman has recently come to this city with her three children.

HADRIAN. Of what sex are the children ?

ANTIOCHUS. They are all girls.

HADRIAN. And you think that a handful of women threaten danger to the state ?

ANTIOCHUS. I do, and very grave danger.

HADRIAN. Of what kind ?

ANTIOCHUS. A disturbance of the peace.

HADRIAN. How ?

ANTIOCHUS. What disturbs the peace and harmony of states more than religious differences ?

HADRIAN. I grant you that. The whole Roman Empire witnesses to the serious troubles they can cause. The body politic is infected by the corpses of slaughtered Christians.

ANTIOCHUS. This woman of whom I speak is urging the people of this country to abandon the religion of their fathers and embrace the Christian faith.

HADRIAN. But have her words any effect ?

ANTIOCHUS. Indeed they have. Our wives hate and scorn us to such an extent that they will not deign to eat with us, still less share our beds.

HADRIAN. This is a real danger, I admit.

ANTIOCHUS. You must protect yourself.

HADRIAN. That stands to reason. Let the woman be brought before me, and I will examine her and see what can be done.

ANTIOCHUS. You wish me to summon her?
HADRIAN. I have said it.

SCENE II

ANTIOCHUS. Foreign woman, what is your name?
SAPIENTIA. Sapientia.
ANTIOCHUS. The Emperor Hadrian orders you
to present yourself at the palace.
SAPIENTIA. I am not afraid to go. I have a noble
escort in my daughters. Nor do I tremble at the thought
of meeting your scowling Emperor face to face.
ANTIOCHUS. It is the way of you Christian rabble
to defy authority.
SAPIENTIA. We acknowledge the authority of Him
Who rules the world; we know that He will not let His
subjects be vanquished.
ANTIOCHUS. Not so much talk. To the palace.
SAPIENTIA. Go before us and show the way. We
will follow you.

SCENE III

ANTIOCHUS. That is the Emperor you see there,
seated on his throne. Be careful what you say to him.
SAPIENTIA. The word of Christ forbids us to take
thought as to what we ought to say. His wisdom is
sufficient for us.
HADRIAN. Are you there, Antiochus?

ANTIOCHUS. At your service, my lord.

HADRIAN. Are these the women whom you have arrested on account of their Christian opinions?

ANTIOCHUS. Yes, lord.

HADRIAN. I am amazed at their beauty; I cannot help admiring their noble and dignified manner.

ANTIOCHUS. Waste no time in admiring them, my lord. Make them worship the gods.

HADRIAN. It would be wiser to ask it as a favour to me at first. Then they may yield.

ANTIOCHUS. That may be best. This frail sex is easily moved by flattery.

HADRIAN. Noble matron, if you desire to enjoy my friendship, I ask you in all gentleness to join me in an act of worship of the gods.

SAPIENTIA. We have no desire for your friendship. And we refuse to worship your gods.

HADRIAN. You will try in vain to rouse my anger. I feel no indignation against you. I appeal to you and your daughters as lovingly as if I were their own father.

SAPIENTIA. My children are not to be cozened by such diabolical flattery. They scorn it as I do.

FAITH. Yes, and laugh at it in our hearts.

ANTIOCHUS. What are you muttering there?

SAPIENTIA. I was speaking to my daughters.

HADRIAN. I judge from appearances that you are of noble race, but I would know more—to what country and family you belong, and your name.

SAPIENTIA. Although we take no pride in it, I come of noble stock.

HADRIAN. That is easy to believe.

SAPIENTIA. My parents were princes of Greece, and I am called Sapientia.

HADRIAN. The splendour of your ancestry is blazoned in your face, and the wisdom of your name sparkles on your lips.

SAPIENTIA. You need not waste your breath in flattering us. We are not to be conquered by fair speeches.

HADRIAN. Why have you left your own people and come to live here ?

SAPIENTIA. For no other reason than that we wished to know the truth. I came to learn more of the faith which you persecute, and to consecrate my daughters to Christ.

HADRIAN. Tell me their names.

SAPIENTIA. The eldest is called Faith, the second Hope, the youngest Charity.

HADRIAN. And how old are they ?

SAPIENTIA. What do you say, children ?   Shall I puzzle his dull brain with some problems in arithmetic ?

FAITH. Do, mother.   It will give us joy to hear you.

SAPIENTIA. As you wish to know the ages of my children, O Emperor, Charity has lived a diminished evenly even number of years ; Hope a number also diminished, but evenly uneven ; and Faith an augmented number, unevenly even.

HADRIAN. Your answer leaves me in ignorance.

SAPIENTIA. That is not surprising, since not one number, but many, come under this definition.

HADRIAN. Explain more clearly, otherwise how can I follow you ?

SAPIENTIA. Charity has now completed two olympiads, Hope two lustres, and Faith three olympiads.

HADRIAN. I am curious to know why the number " 8," which is two olympiads, and the number " 10," which is two lustres, are called " diminished " ; also why the number " 12," which is made up of three olympiads, is said to be " augmented."

SAPIENTIA. Every number is said to be " diminished " the parts of which when added together give a sum which is less than the number of which they are parts. Such a number is 8. For the half of 8 is 4, the quarter of 8 is 2, and the eighth of 8 is 1 ; and these added together give 7. It is the same with 10. Its half is 5, its fifth part 2, its tenth part 1, and these added together give 8. On the other hand, a number is said to be " augmented " when its parts added together exceed it. Such, for instance, is 12. Its half is 6, its third 4, its fourth 3, its sixth 2, its twelfth 1, and the sum of these figures 16. And in accordance with the principle which decrees that between all excesses shall rule the exquisite proportion of the mean, that number is called " perfect " the sum of the parts of which is equal to its whole. Such a number is 6, whose parts—a third, a half, and a sixth—

added together, come to 6.   For the same reason 28, 496, and 8000 are called " perfect."

HADRIAN. And what of the other numbers ?

SAPIENTIA. They are all either augmented or diminished.

HADRIAN. And that " evenly even " number of which you spoke ?

SAPIENTIA. That is one which can be divided into two equal parts, and these parts again into two equal parts, and so on in succession until we come to indivisible unity : 8 and 16 and all numbers obtained by doubling them are examples.

HADRIAN. Continue.   We have not heard yet of the " evenly uneven " number.

SAPIENTIA. One which can be divided by two, but the parts of which after that are indivisible : 10 is such a number, and all others obtained by doubling odd numbers.   They differ from the " evenly even " numbers because in them only the minor term can be divided, whereas in the " evenly even " the major term is also capable of division.   In the first type, too, all the parts are evenly even in name and in quantity, whereas in the second type when the division is even the quotient is uneven, and *vice versa*.

HADRIAN. I am not familiar with these terms, and divisors and quotients alike mean nothing to me.*

* It has been my duty to preserve this rather tiresome numerical discourse, which no doubt Roswitha

SAPIENTIA. When numbers of any magnitude are set down in order, the first set down is called the " minor term " and the last the " major." When, in making a division, we say by how many the number is to be divided, we give the " divisor," but when we enumerate how many there are in each of the parts we set forth the " quotient."

HADRIAN. And the " unevenly even " numbers ?

SAPIENTIA. They, like the " evenly even," can be halved, not only once, but sometimes twice, thrice, and even four times, but not down to indivisible unity.

HADRIAN. Little did I think that a simple question as to the age of these children could give rise to such an intricate and unprofitable dissertation.

SAPIENTIA. It would be unprofitable if it did not lead us to appreciate the wisdom of our Creator, and the wondrous knowledge of the Author of the world, Who in the beginning created the world out of nothing, and set everything in number, measure, and weight, and then, in time and the age of man, formulated a science which reveals fresh wonders the more we study it.

introduced to impress the " learned men " to whom she submitted her work, because it throws an interesting light on the studies pursued in such a monastery as Gandersheim in the 10th century. Equivalent modern English terms have been employed where the original, by change of usage, has become misleading. For example, " divisor " and " quotient " have been substituted for " denomination " and " quantity."

HADRIAN. I had my reasons for enduring your lecture with patience. I hope to persuade you to submit.

SAPIENTIA. To what?

HADRIAN. To worshipping the gods.

SAPIENTIA. That we can never do.

HADRIAN. Take warning. If you are obstinate, you will be put to the torture.

SAPIENTIA. It is in your power to kill the body, but you will not succeed in harming the soul.

ANTIOCHUS. The day has passed, and the night is falling. This is no time to argue. Supper is ready.

HADRIAN. Let these women be taken to the prison near our palace, and give them three days to reflect.

ANTIOCHUS. Soldiers, see that these women are well guarded and given no chance of escape.

SCENE IV

SAPIENTIA. Oh, my dearest ones! My beloved children! Do not let this narrow prison sadden you. Do not be frightened by the threat of sufferings to come.

FAITH. Our weak bodies may dread the torture, but our souls look forward with joy to the reward.

SAPIENTIA. You are only children, but your understanding is ripe and strong. It will triumph over your tender years.

HOPE. You must help us with your prayers. Then we shall conquer.

SAPIENTIA. This I pray without ceasing, this I implore—that you may stand firm in the faith which I instilled into you while you were infants at my breast.

CHARITY. Can we forget what we learned there ? Never.

SAPIENTIA. I gave you milk. I nourished and cherished you, that I might wed you to a heavenly bridegroom, not to an earthly one. I trusted that for your dear sakes I might be deemed worthy of being received into the family of the Eternal King.

FAITH. For His love we are all ready to die.

SAPIENTIA. Oh, children, your words are sweeter to me than nectar !

HOPE. When we come before the tribunal you will see what courage our love will give us.

SAPIENTIA. Your mother will be crowned by your virginity and glorified by your martyrdom.

CHARITY. Let us go hand in hand to the tyrant and make him feel ashamed.

SAPIENTIA. We must wait till the hour comes when we are summoned.

FAITH. We chafe at the delay, but we must be patient.

SCENE V

HADRIAN. Antiochus, bring the Greek prisoners before us.

ANTIOCHUS. Step forward, Sapientia. The Emperor has asked for you and your daughters.

SAPIENTIA. Walk with me bravely, children, and persevere with one mind in the faith. Think only of the happiness before you—of the martyr's palm.

HOPE. We are ready. And He is with us for Whose love we are to be led to death.

HADRIAN. The three days' respite which of our clemency we granted you is over. If you have profited by it, obey our commands.

SAPIENTIA. We have profited by it. It has strengthened our determination not to yield.

ANTIOCHUS. It is beneath your dignity to bandy words with this obstinate woman. Have you not had enough of her insolence and presumption?

HADRIAN. Am I to send her away unpunished?

ANTIOCHUS. By no means.

HADRIAN. What then?

ANTIOCHUS. Address yourself to the little girls. If they defy you, do not spare them because of their tender years, but have them put to death. That will teach their obstinate mother a lesson.

HADRIAN. I will do as you advise.

ANTIOCHUS. This way you will succeed.

HADRIAN. Faith, there is the venerated statue of the great Diana. Carry a libation to the holy goddess, and you will win her favour.

FAITH. What a foolish man the Emperor must be to give such an order!

HADRIAN. What are you muttering there? Behave yourself and do not laugh.

FAITH. How can I help laughing? Such a lack of wisdom is ludicrous.

HADRIAN. Whose lack of wisdom?

FAITH. Why, yours!

ANTIOCHUS. You dare to speak to the Emperor so!

FAITH. I speak the truth.

ANTIOCHUS. This is not to be endured!

FAITH. What is it but folly to tell us to insult the Creator of the world and worship a bit of metal!

ANTIOCHUS. This girl is crazy—a raving lunatic! She calls the ruler of the world a fool!

FAITH. I have said it, and I am ready to repeat it. I shall not take back my words as long as I live.

ANTIOCHUS. That will not be long. You deserve to die at once for such impudence.

FAITH. I wish for nothing better than death in Christ.

HADRIAN. Enough of this! Let ten centurions take turns in flaying her with scourges.

ANTIOCHUS. She deserves it.

HADRIAN. Most valiant centurions, approach, and wipe out the insult which has been offered us.

ANTIOCHUS. That is the way.

HADRIAN. Ask her now, Antiochus, if she will yield.

ANTIOCHUS. Faith, will you now withdraw your

insults to the Imperial Majesty, and promise not to repeat them ?

FAITH. Why now ?

ANTIOCHUS. The scourging should have brought you to your senses.

FAITH. These whips cannot silence me, as they do not hurt at all.

ANTIOCHUS. Cursed obstinacy ! Was there ever such insolence ?

HADRIAN. Although her body weakens under the chastisement, her spirit is still swollen with pride.

FAITH. Hadrian, you are wrong. It is not I who am weakening, but your executioners. They sweat and faint with fatigue.

HADRIAN. Antiochus, tell them to cut the nipples off her breasts. The shame will cow her.

ANTIOCHUS. I care not about the means, so long as she is forced to yield.

FAITH. You have wounded my pure breast, but you have not hurt me. And look ! Instead of blood a stream of milk gushes from my wounds.

HADRIAN. Put her on a gridiron, and let fire be placed beneath so that she may be roasted to death.

ANTIOCHUS. She deserves a terrible death for her boldness in defying you.

FAITH. All you do to cause me suffering is a source of bliss to me. I am as happy on this gridiron as if it were a little boat at sea !

HADRIAN. Bring a brazier full of pitch and wax, and place it on the fire. Then fling this rebellious girl into the boiling liquid.

FAITH. I will leap into it joyfully of my own accord.

HADRIAN. So be it.

FAITH. I laugh at your threats. Look! Am I hurt? I am swimming merrily in the boiling pitch. Its fierce heat seems as cool to me as the morning dew.

HADRIAN. Antiochus, what can we do with her?

ANTIOCHUS. She must not escape.

HADRIAN. She shall be beheaded.

ANTIOCHUS. That seems the only way of conquering her.

FAITH. Now let my soul rejoice and exult in the Lord.

SAPIENTIA. O Christ, invincible Conqueror of Satan, give my child, Faith, endurance to the end!

FAITH. Holy and dear mother, say a last farewell to your daughter. Kiss your firstborn, but do not mourn for me, for my hands are outstretched to the reward of eternity.

SAPIENTIA. Oh, my daughter, my darling dear, I am not dismayed—I am not distressed! I bid you farewell rejoicing. I kiss your mouth and eyes, weeping for joy. My only prayer is that beneath the executioner's sword you may keep the mystery of your name inviolate.

FAITH. Oh, my sisters, born of the same womb,

give me the kiss of peace, and prepare yourselves for the struggle !

HOPE. Help us with your prayers. Pray with all your might that we may be found worthy to follow in your footsteps.

FAITH. Listen to the words of our holy mother. She has always taught us to despise the things of earth that we may gain those which are eternal.

CHARITY. We shall obey her in everything. We want to be worthy of eternal joy.

FAITH. Come, executioner, do your duty, and put an end to my life.

SAPIENTIA. I embrace the severed head of my dead child, and as I cover it with kisses I praise Thee, O Christ, Who hast given the victory to a little maid.

HADRIAN. Hope, listen to me. Believe me, I advise you with fatherly affection.

HOPE. What advice do you give me ?

HADRIAN. I beg you not to imitate your misguided sister. I would not have you undergo the same torture.

HOPE. Would that I were worthy to imitate her sufferings, and so win a reward like hers !

HADRIAN. Do not harden your young heart, but give way and burn incense before great Diana. Then I will adopt you as my own child, and love you most tenderly.

HOPE. I should not care to have you for a father,

and I want no favours from you. You deceive yourself with vain hopes if you suppose that I shall submit.

HADRIAN. Be more careful in your speech or you will make me angry.

HOPE. Be angry. What is it to me?

ANTIOCHUS. I am amazed, Augustus, that you should tolerate for a moment such insolence from a pert little child! I boil with indignation that she should be allowed such licence.

HADRIAN. I wished to be merciful to her youth, but I can no longer be indulgent. She shall be punished as she deserves.

ANTIOCHUS. I wish that were possible.

HADRIAN. Come, lictors, and scourge this little rebel to death with your heaviest rods.

ANTIOCHUS. She deserves to feel the full weight of your anger, as she has mocked your gracious clemency.

HOPE. Here is the only clemency for which I long— here the only mercy I crave.

ANTIOCHUS. Sapientia, what are you murmuring there, standing with uplifted eyes by the body of your dead child?

SAPIENTIA. I am imploring Almighty God to give Hope the same firm courage that He gave Faith.

HOPE. Oh, mother, mother! How wonderful are your prayers! Even as you prayed the uplifted hands of the panting executioners became powerless. I have not felt a twinge of pain.

HADRIAN. So you do not mind scourging ! We will try some sharper torture.

HOPE. The most savage and deadly you can invent ! The more cruelty you show the greater will be your humiliation.

HADRIAN. Let her be suspended in the air, and lacerated with nails until her bowels gush forth, and the skin is stripped from her bones. Break her to pieces limb by limb.

ANTIOCHUS. That order is worthy of an emperor. The punishment fits the crime.

HOPE. Oh, Antiochus, you are as crafty as a fox, but you flatter with the cunning of a chameleon.

ANTIOCHUS. Be quiet, you wretch ! I thank the gods you will soon not have a mouth to prattle with.

HOPE. It will not be as you hope. Both you and your master will be put to confusion.

HADRIAN. What is this strange sweetness in the air ? If I am not mistaken a marvellous perfume fills the room.

HOPE. O Emperor, the torn shreds of my flesh are giving forth a heavenly fragrance to make you admit that you have no power to hurt me by torture !

HADRIAN. Antiochus, advise me.

ANTIOCHUS. We must think of some other punishment.

HADRIAN. Put in the brazier a vessel full of oil and wax and pitch. Bind her and throw her in.

ANTIOCHUS. Yes, she will not find it so easy to escape from Vulcan.

HOPE. Christ has before now made fire grow mild and change its nature.

HADRIAN. Antiochus, what is that sound? I seem to hear a noise like that of rushing waters.

ANTIOCHUS. My lord! My lord!

HADRIAN. What has happened?

ANTIOCHUS. The boiling fire has burst the cauldron! It has overflowed and consumed every man near it. Only the vile witch who caused the disaster has escaped unhurt.

HADRIAN. It seems we are worsted.

ANTIOCHUS. Yes, we can do nothing.

HADRIAN. She must be beheaded like the other.

ANTIOCHUS. By the sword only can she be destroyed.

HOPE. Charity, my dear, my only sister, have no fear of the tyrant's threats, and do not wince at the thought of suffering. Be strong in faith, and strive to follow the example of your sisters who are going before you to the palace of heaven.

CHARITY. I am weary of this earth. I do not want to be separated from you even for a short time.

HOPE. Have courage! Stretch out your hands to the palm. We shall be separated only for a moment. Soon, very soon, we shall be together in heaven.

CHARITY. Soon! Soon!

HOPE. Be joyful, noble mother! Do not grieve for me. You should laugh, not weep, to see me die for Christ.

SAPIENTIA. Indeed I do rejoice, but my joy will be full only when your little sister has followed you, slain in the same way—and when my turn comes, mine last of all.

HOPE. The blessed Trinity will give you back your three children.

SAPIENTIA. Courage, my child! The executioner comes towards us with drawn sword.

HOPE. Welcome, sword! Do Thou, O Christ, receive my soul driven from its bodily mansion for the confession of Thy Name.

SAPIENTIA. Oh, Charity, lovely offspring of my womb, the one hope of my bosom, do not disappoint your mother who expects you to win this last fight! Despise safety now, and you will attain the same glory which shines on your sisters, and, like them, wear the crown of unspotted virginity.

CHARITY. Support me with your holy prayers, mother. Pray that I may be worthy to share their joy.

SAPIENTIA. Stand fast in the faith to the end, and your reward will be an everlasting holiday.

HADRIAN. Now, little Charity. Your sisters' insolence has exhausted my patience and exasperated me. I want no more long speeches. I shall not waste much time on you.   Obey my commands, and you shall enjoy all the good things this life has to offer. Disobey, and evil will fall on you.

CHARITY. I long for the good things. I will not have the evil.

HADRIAN. That pleases me, and you shall profit by it.   I will be indulgent and set you an easy task.

CHARITY. What is it ?

HADRIAN. You shall say " Great is Diana." That is all. I will not compel you to sacrifice.

CHARITY. I will not say it.

HADRIAN. Why ?

CHARITY. Because I will not tell a lie. My sisters and I were born of the same parents, instructed in the same mysteries, and confirmed in the same faith. We have the same wish, the same understanding, the same resolution. Therefore, I am never likely to differ from them in anything.

ANTIOCHUS. Oh, what an insult—to be defied by a mere doll !

CHARITY. Although I am small, my reason is big enough to put you to shame.

HADRIAN. Take her away, Antiochus, and have her stretched on the rack and whipped.

ANTIOCHUS. I fear that stripes will be of no use.

HADRIAN. Then order a furnace to be heated for three days and three nights, and let her be cast into the flames.

CHARITY. A mighty man ! He cannot conquer a child of eight without calling in fire to help him !

HADRIAN. Go, Antiochus, and see that my orders are carried out.

CHARITY. He may pretend to obey to satisfy your cruelty, but he will not be able to hurt me. Stripes will not wound my body, and the flames will not singe my hair or my garments.

HADRIAN. We shall see.

CHARITY. Yes, we shall see.

SCENE VI

HADRIAN. What is wrong, Antiochus ? Why have you returned, and with such a dejected air ?

ANTIOCHUS. When you know the reason, you will be dejected too.

HADRIAN. Come, what is it ?

ANTIOCHUS. That little vixen whom you handed over to me to be tortured was first scourged in my presence, and I swear that not so much as the surface of her delicate skin was grazed. Then I had her cast into the fiery furnace which glowed scarlet with the tremendous heat.

HADRIAN. Enough ! Come to the point.

ANTIOCHUS. The flames belched forth, and five thousand men were burned to death.

HADRIAN. And what happened to her ?

ANTIOCHUS. You mean to Charity?

HADRIAN. Who else?

ANTIOCHUS. She ran to and fro, playing in the fierce whirlwind of smoke and flame, and sang praises to her God. Those who watched closely said that three men dressed in white walked by her side.

HADRIAN. I blush to see her again, as I have not been able to harm her.

ANTIOCHUS. She must perish by the sword like the others.

HADRIAN. Let us use it then, and without delay.

SCENE VII

ANTIOCHUS. Uncover that obstinate little neck, Charity, and prepare for the sword of the executioner.

CHARITY. This time I do not wish to resist. I am glad to obey.

SAPIENTIA. Now, little one, now we must give thanks; now we must exult in Christ. Now I am free from anxiety, for I am certain of your triumph.

CHARITY. Kiss me, mother, and commend my soul to Christ.

SAPIENTIA. May He Who quickened you in my womb receive the spirit He breathed into you!

CHARITY. Glory be to Thee, O Christ, Who hast called me to Thyself, and honoured me with the martyr's crown!

SAPIENTIA. Farewell, beloved child, farewell; and

when you are united to Christ in heaven give a thought
to the mother who gave you life even when the years
had exhausted her strength.

SCENE VIII

SAPIENTIA. Noble matrons, gather round me, and
help me bury the bodies of my children.

MATRONS. We will strew herbs and spices on their
little bodies, and solemnize their funeral rites with
ceremony.

SAPIENTIA. Great is the generosity and wonderful
the kindness you show to me and my dead.

MATRONS. We would do anything to relieve your
pain.

SAPIENTIA. I know it.

MATRONS. What place have you chosen for their
burial ?

SAPIENTIA. It is three miles outside the city. I hope
that is not too far for you ?

MATRONS. By no means. We will follow their
bodies to the place you have chosen.

SCENE IX

SAPIENTIA. This is the place.

MATRONS. It is well chosen. The very spot to
keep the relics of these blessed martyrs !

SAPIENTIA. O Earth, I commit my precious little flowers to thy keeping! O Earth, cherish them in thy spacious bosom until they spring forth again at the resurrection more glorious and fair! O Christ, fill their souls with light, and give rest and peace to their bones!

MATRONS. Amen.

SAPIENTIA. I thank you all from my heart for the comfort you have brought me since my loss.

MATRONS. Would you like us to remain here with you?

SAPIENTIA. I thank you, no.

MATRONS. Why not?

SAPIENTIA. Because your health will suffer if you fatigue yourselves further on my account. Have you not done enough in watching with me three days. Depart in peace. Return home happy.

MATRONS. Will you not come with us?

SAPIENTIA. I cannot.

MATRONS. What, then, is your plan?

SAPIENTIA. I shall stay here in the hope that my petition will be granted, and that what I most desire will come to pass.

MATRONS. What is that petition? What do you desire?

SAPIENTIA. This only—that when my prayer is ended I may die in Christ.

MATRONS. Will you not let us stay to the end, then, and give you burial?

SAPIENTIA. As you please.

O Adonai Emmanuel, begotten by the Divine Creator of all things before time began, and born in time of a Virgin Mother—O Thou Who in Thy dual nature remainest most wonderfully one Christ, the unity of person not being divided by the diversity of natures, nor yet the diversity of natures confounded in the unity of person—to Thee let the serene angelic choir, singing in sweet harmony with the spheres, raise an exultant song! Let all created things praise Thee, because Thou Who alone with the Holy Ghost art form without matter, by the will of the Father and the co-operation of the Spirit didst deign to become man, passible like men, yet impassible like God. O Thou Who didst not shrink from tasting death and destroyed it by Thy Resurrection that none who believe in Thee should perish, but know eternal life, on Thee I call! I do not forget that Thou, perfect God yet true man, didst promise that those who for Thy sake renounced their earthly possessions would be rewarded a hundredfold and receive the gift of eternal life. Inspired by that promise, Thou seest that I have done what I could; of my own free will, and for Thy sake, I have sacrificed the children I bore. Oh, in Thy goodness do not delay the fulfilment of Thy promise, but free me swiftly from the bonds of this flesh that I may see my children and rejoice with them. Grant me the joy of hearing them sing the new song as they follow Thee, O Lamb of the Virgin! Let me be gladdened by their glory, and although I may not like them chant the mystical song of virginity, let me praise Thee, Who art not Thyself the Father, yet art of the same substance as the Father, with Whom and with the Holy Ghost, one Lord of the whole world, one King of all things upon the earth and in the heights above and the deeps below, Thou dost reign and rule for ever and ever !

MATRONS. O Lord, receive her soul ! Amen.

A NOTE ON THE ACTING
OF THE PLAYS

THE evidence that Roswitha's plays were intended for representation has already been discussed. If they were ever acted in her own time at Gandersheim by members of the community, we need not assume that the performances were ludicrously artless. We have only to read contemporary descriptions of the celebrations of great feasts in monasteries in the so-called " dark ages," or to observe how strong is the element of significant and controlled " action " in the ceremonial of the Catholic Church as it exists to-day, to imagine that people accustomed to take part in these dramatic services would have little difficulty in giving an impressive performance of a religious play. Even if we discard the theory that such performances took place, an imaginative conception of what they might have been like will save us, if we desire to act these plays now, from adopting an exaggeratedly primitive method. It is our duty to do our best for them, neglecting no means of emphasizing their dramatic strength and helping their dramatic weakness. As we have no authority in a known " convention " to guide us, the least we can do is to refrain from inventing a comically crude one based on an arrogant condescension to past ignorance of what in any century is dramatically effective.

When *Callimachus* was brought on to the modern stage a misleading impression of Roswitha's ability as a dramatist was created by a calculated childishness in the interpretation. All the characters were kept in view of the audience whether they were concerned in a scene or not, and the end of each scene was marked, as the end of an over is marked in cricket, by a general change in positions. Roswitha's piety was held up to ridicule, and her glorification of chastity burlesqued to the satisfaction of those to whom jokes at the expense of old-fashioned virtues never fail to appeal. Drusiana's prayer that she might die rather than yield to Callimachus was greeted with shouts of laughter. And it was said that the mirth was natural and

inevitable because Roswitha's manner is so naïve! Yet
if she is treated on her merits, not as an archaic freak,
she can be impressive enough on the stage as Edith
Craig's production of *Paphnutius* proved. In this production the abrupt transition from scene to scene was
bridged by the singing of plainsong melodies, derived
from MSS. of the ninth century. The suggestions for
action in the lines were examined with sympathetic insight, and developed with imagination. The actors and
actresses took their task seriously and used all their
skill in making the characters live. The old story of the
conversion of Thais became new, and although many
found Roswitha's treatment of it unpalatable, none found
it ludicrous. A comparison of the divergent impressions
made by the Roswitha of *Callimachus* and the Roswitha
of *Paphnutius* is a lesson in the difficulty of sifting what
the dramatist has done from what the interpreter has done,
a difficulty all the greater when the text of a play is not
available. Now that *Callimachus* can be read it will be
easier for those who saw its solitary performance to
recognize that it was travestied on the stage.

Imagination, sympathy with Roswitha's uncompromising religious faith, a few sets of curtains, or an
interchangeable scene, actors capable either by nature
or training of extracting a pound of effect out of an ounce
of dialogue, are the foundations on which performances
of these plays can be built. *Paphnutius*, *Abraham*, and
Callimachus are obviously more actable than the others,
but I feel that a great deal might be done with *Sapientia*.
Perhaps one day it will be possible to arrange a Roswitha
" cycle " for the edification of a few enthusiasts. Meanwhile those who share my belief that plays are not plays
until they are acted, can amuse themselves by thinking
over different methods of representation.